THE NEW HUMANISM

THE NEW HUMANISM

Conversations on the North Campus

MAX HAMBURGH, Ph.D.

CITY COLLEGE OF NEW YORK

and

ALBERT EINSTEIN COLLEGE OF MEDICINE

PHILOSOPHICAL LIBRARY

New York

Except where otherwise stated all the opinions and all the views and ideas expressed in this book are strictly and solely those of the author. He and he alone takes full responsibility for these views.

Printed in the United States of America

This book is dedicated, first and foremost, to my wife, Traude, from whom I stole the many hours spent in writing this book and without whose companionship and love I would not have been able to live through the difficult years which provoked me to write it.

This book is also dedicated to the few people left who knew me when I was very young — Carl, Illa, Else, Lona — and to my children, Mark and Annette, and to the many people who have been good to me in my life whom I can name affectionately only in my heart.

CONTENTS

PREFACE

Americans have gone in for self-analysis in a big way during the last two decades and a half, and the mirrors they have been putting up to themselves have not all been complimentary or reassuring to them. Those of us, who, like Dean Acheson have also been "present at the creation" of the so-called post war world, though in less commanding position than the former Secretary of State, when looking back over the 30 years that have elapsed since VE Day and VJ Day note with amazement the endless stream of self-reviews end self-appraisals that continue to arrive on the literary market in never-ending succession. After reading some of these exercises in self-reflection, I am tempted to predict that if a mirror could be queried, "Mirror, mirror on the wall, who is the fairest of them all," it would prefer to take the 5th Amendment.

One wonders about the reasons that motivate us to examine everything from the way we love, raise children, buy, work, pray, and die. For a nation that has always prided itself on being extrovert rather than introvert, the excessive preoccupation with ourselves is a new phenomenon. Maybe our generation (the over 40 crowd) experienced a vague feeling of discomfort that something has eluded them since they came back from the war to reach out and find their places in the brave new world. Those of us who managed to break into the middle class, whether lower middle or upper, know that we have more money now than we ever dreamt of having and that we can afford more of the so-called good things of life than we ever hoped to acquire. But some undefined and undefinable anxiety persists, reminding us that the promise of the great new world

1

which we thought was within our grasp on VE and VJ Days somehow eluded us. This "Unbehagen in der Kultur" has taken different forms and stimulated different responses. For the more timid and sentimental souls among us, the escape into nostalgia provides a pleasant and easily available remedy that quiets the fears that are aroused by all those disturbing voices that block the return to the 19th century.

The more aggressive and more action-minded personalities are ready to do battle and to pick up the gauntlets, and to repulse the attacks head on that are made on the values of the past. They, too, perceive a changed world which has brought little fulfillment to their hopes. They don't like being short-changed, but they blame the youth, the college kids, the long-hairs, the liberals and the radicals and all their allies for defying and challenging authority. What they confuse in their minds is that the inadequacy and disorder of their surroundings is not the making of those who protested, but that the protests were stimulated by an environment that has been unusually harsh and totally lacking in compassion to some of them.

The more educated members of our society, on the other hand, have invested a good deal of their time, dollars and efforts to review, evaluate, analyze, and explain their attitudes, morals, mores, customs, habits, hangups, and our social and political behavior and misbehavior, past and present and future. Reference is made to such books as:

1. "The Lonely Crowd" by David Reisman
2. "Individualism Reconstructed" by David Reisman
3. "Mirror for man" by Clayde Klukholm
4. "The Organization Man" by W. Whyte
5. "The Hidden Persuaders"; "The Waste Makers" "The Status Seekers"; "The Pyramid Climbers" by Vance Packard 6. "The Feminine Mystique" by Betty Friedan
7. "Future Shock" by Alvin Toffler
8. "The Greening of America" by C. A. Reich

9. "Tomorrow is Already Here" by R. Jungk
10. "The Shook Up Generation" by H. E. Salisbury
11. "The Affluent Society" by J. K. Galbraith
12. "Making It" by N. Podhoretz

In 1952, writing in praise of David Reisman's "The Lonely Crowd," Lionel Trilling remarked:

> "Contemporary social science was developing an increasingly acute and subtle 'sense of social actuality' which contemporary literature lacked. Indeed, sociology seemed to be in the process of taking over from literature one of literature's most characteristic functions, the investigation and criticism of morals and manners.

> "Twenty years later, this process has gone farther than anyone could foresee. Where our parents and grandparents once turned to novelists, we find ourselves more and more apt to turn toward sociologists, anthropologists, and psychologists, for light on the way we live now."[1]

My objection to these books is only minor. I think many of them are too long to be read, and long books, as a rule, are more likely to be placed *on* the bookshelves than *off* it. There is another disadvantage to long books, aside from the fact that half the number of pages would suffice to prove their point. Long books by their very effort to be exhaustive give an image of authority and, therefore, tend to intimidate rather than encourage the reader to exercise his own power of thought, or to reply in debate. Free flow of goods can be promoted easier if they are movable. Ideas can be exchanged best if they are not too heavily packed.

---

*Quoted from a book review by Marshal Berman in the New York Times Book Review, February 27, 1972.

3

This author does not wish to add to the considerable literary output already accumulated, although he feels that the last word about the meaning and the root and origin of the "new culture" and the contamination of the adult culture by the new has not yet been said by such best sellers as William Reisch's "Greening of America." The focusing of many and diverse minds on the same subject deserves to be encouraged. I, myself, feel a little bit uneasy in the role of a 50-year-old professor trying to explain the message of the young. I think the young are sufficiently eloquent by themselves and not in need of my efforts at translation. However, if the so-called new outlook, whatever is meant by that, were really only a "youth culture," it would not even be deserving of so much attention by men as old as myself. Granted that the young are the most vociferous and most outspoken public relations people for what passes as the "new mood" or the "new outlook," many of its basic assumptions are shared by people much older than the 18 to 25 year crowd. That, plus the prediction that at least some of the new ideals now so passionately defended by the young, will remain to influence their attitudes in the not-so-distant future when they, themselves, will move into positions vacated by those setting the tone now, makes their ideas, attitudes and outlooks worthy of continued probing and analysis, and above all understanding without necessarily giving assent to all of them.

At the risk of boring prospective readers who have been overfed by too many critiques of our morals, mores, and manners, I shall try to say what I feel deserves adding in as concise and crisp a manner as I know how. I beg the reader to judge the following essays as attempts to come to grips with some of the more important books about themselves that have come to disturb our complacency. Books are, after all, not only published in order to stimulate the minds of reviewers. The mental circuits they trigger in the minds of the general reading public is really their ultimate payoff and both publisher and author deserve some feedback of how their labor affected the minds

4

of those to whom their words and thoughts were addressed. The list of titles that triggered the mental processes of this author is long and varied. Some of them exerted greater influence than others and some are accordingly judged arbitrarily by this author as more important than others. This judgment is admittedly subjective. If I were to establish a hierarchy of the most profound volumes, I would list the following titles, not necessarily in the order of their importance.

1. "The Greening of America" by C. A. Reich
2. "Beyond Freedom and Dignity" by B. F. Skinner
3. "Without Marx or Jesus" by J. F. Revel
4. "Power and Innocence" by Rollo May
5. "The Naked Ape" and "The Human Zoo" by D. Morris
6. "On Aggression" by Konrad Lorenz
7. "The Dark Night of Resistance" by D. Berrigan
8. "Coming Apart" by W. L. O'Neill
9. "The Lonely Crowd" and "Individualism Reconstructed" by D. Reisman
10. "365 Days" by R. J. Glasser
11. "Don't Shoot We Are Your Children" by J. A. Lucas
12. "A Theory of Justice" by J. Rawls

In a sense the present collection of essays is an intensely personal document that attempts to describe how one professor and a group of middle class students experienced some of the new ideas and attitudes that were generated by these books and how the mental and emotional circuits were aroused by contact with some of the books that were placed on the above private "best seller list."

For many of us, particularly on campus, the last decade was an intellectual adventure. Few can remember it with a great sense of nostalgia, but adventure it was, nevertheless. Like on a search zeroing in on a target, our thoughts turned and returned in concentric circles to the same problems, such as "the war" and "the nature of good and evil," "the nature of man" and "whether he can be good," "whether he can preserve his freedom," and "how he can meet his responsibilities in a complex society." These topics were debated in endless "bull sessions" that were spiced sometimes with a drink but never a drug. Most of the intellectual circuitry that was let loose was actually triggered from the books cited above.

I am not going to fall into the trap of the numbers game and will not try to estimate the extent to which the intellectual and emotional odyssey that I am describing was shared by a representative and statiscally significant segment of the campus population as a whole, or whether the group in whose experiences I participated represents so skewed a sample that it is representative of no one but myself.

Like in the fable of "Rashomon" where three different eyewitnesses each gave a different account of the same event, so the story of the changes in mood and attitudes that have happened all around us can only be fully comprehended if many different observers tell their own version. Events, such as the emergence of a new "Welt or Lebensauschaung," or the setting of a new mood are much too complex for objective reporting by one single individual.

In spite of all the lip service that is being paid to "individualism" or to "doing one's own thing," nobody wants to write a book that is essentially and exclusively a personal document. One's own thoughts, ideas and outlooks gain significance and are considered worthy to be transcribed into linotype only if and when they offer something of near universal relevance or when they are representative of or part of a more collective intellectual ownership. This writer is not going to fall into the trap of presenting himself as a spokesman for anybody but himself. On the other hand, there is no use denying that the ideas and outlooks, the attitudes and hopes described in the succeeding chapters were turned on by the intellectual exchanges that were carried on with many people, primarily students and colleagues on the campus of the City College of New York during the last decade.

The City College which is the academic home of this author has a rather peculiar geography. We distinguish between the North Campus and the South Campus, but the distinction is more than a territorial one. The border separating the North Campus from the South Campus is, perhaps, symbolic of the invisible line separating the whole national student body into two populations that differ in outlook, tastes and aspirations but still have enough contact to rub off their differing ideas on one another. The North Campus contains the buildings where science and engineering and all the courses necessary for the professions are taught. The students who cluster there have indicated, by implication at least, that they expect to remain within the framework of the society, much as they may loathe some of its injustices. The students of the South Campus are attracted more by ideas, some of them far out, that lead them far afield from traditional values. It is on the South Campus that student revolts are made, non-negotiable demands are formulated, and idealistic youths chain themselves to iron gates to move what they perceive to be the mighty of the world whom they mistakenly identify with the men who run the university. By the time they recognize that the power of the latter is more fiction than fact, they are usually out of college. But the lines that separate the South from the North Campus are fluid; the students pass freely across the border and mingle with one another, as do their ideas and hopes and blueprints for salvation. It is this "symbolic" division that transcends geography to which the subtitle of this book, "Conversations on the North Campus," refers.

The students with whom I conversed were, themselves, a diverse group. They were mostly from middle class families studying in preparation for professional careers, if by that term is meant people who plan to make a living by serving the needs of others with their specialized skills. Many of my partners in debate were Jewish. Some were Catholics, some Quakers and quite a few were agnostics. Most of them were white, some were black, but all of them shared a preference for public service and declared themselves strongly in favor of an expansion of compassion and empathy. They were turned off by the excessive materialism which they judged to be the main defect of their otherwise lovable parents, and all of them are united by a desire for peace.

These sentiments seemed to originate and flourish probably most strongly among the middle class population of American campuses (encompassing both students and professors). There must be reasons for that. Whatever the sins or failures of progressive education may have been, only the children who were raised in the warmth radiated by permissive parents of middle class homes could grow up to "make love their guiding line." People who are early and continually exposed to deprivation, degradation and harassment will at best be attracted to more "sterner ideals." Conversely, a generation that has been drenched in an ocean of commodities and has taken in "La Dolce Vita" along with its bottle has had too much too soon. To them, only "finding oneself" seemed worthwhile, until they discovered that what they found was not worth finding. Only a generation somewhat in between these two extremes, one that enjoyed the good fortune of inhabiting, at least during their formative years, the genteel world of a relatively unrestricted childhood without being drenched in an ocean of affluence, was likely to develop an appetite for more ethereal goods than the wealth, security, comfort and status that was so passionately sought by their well-meaning parents.

It is probably no accident that the people whom I met belonged ideologically to the ranks of the moderates rather than to those of extremists. That does not mean that the extremists did not exist on campus. It just so happened they were as uninteresting to me as I probably was to them. Numerically, the "liberals" probably have a slight edge over the "conservatives" on the campus, but even the ranks of the university conservatives are probably more attuned to the sophistication of a Bill Buckley than to the fundamentalism of a Barry Gold-water or to members of the Birch Society. Activists with strong political convictions, as well as crusaders, of which there was certainly no shortage on the campuses, have nothing but contempt for those who walk the "middle of the road" because, as they say, moderates have too much reluctance to "rock the boat" no matter how inequitable the seating arrangement. As far as they are concerned, moderates are, therefore, hardly worth talking to.

Indeed, we "moderates" had no universal program for salvation — only instinct, and our instincts lead us to distrust *all* doctrines which elevate ideologies above human needs. By instinct, we put our trust into the kind of humanism that tends to diminish human suffering. That is why we could be called both "anti-communists" and "soft on communism" at the same time. It is impossible to be a humanist and not to seek liberation for any people from the most repressive straight jacket ever designed by any set of rulers for its subjects, while at the same time it is inconceivable for a humanist to seek anyone's liberation at a price that would transform slaves into ghosts.

The new humanism that has emerged during the 1960's was essentially a "mood." It was not a blueprint or a program for action, nor a concise system of doctrine, nor a philosophy. The new humanism was an expression of preferences, of tastes, of hopes and aspirations for a better life rather than a well-reasoned proposal for the changes necessary to realize these hopes. It relied more on the hypothalamus than on the cerebral cortex for inspiration.

The discerning reader may find little more than the well known platitudes that can be heard in most sermons at church or synagogue, when pressed for rational expression of how to attain the good life. The only thing that was new was the earnestness about translating the aspirations into working prescriptions for everyday life. Communes, Jesus freaks, peace demonstrators, flower children, agitators in favor of making love — not war, crusaders for nudity, woman's or gay lib — all of

9

them were nourished by the same intellectual, or shall I say hypothalamic, arousal of the longing for more humanity and more humaneness.

I have had some difficulty in understanding the depth of suspicion and anger that was directed at so many of the young, at their often outlandish garb, appearance, habits and tastes. Was it a sense of guilt because they could do so well without some of the creature comforts which have become so dear to the rest of us, so much so that their attainment has practically become the measure of our worth, status and virility? Perhaps the reason for the deep distrust that rank and file Americans still harbor for even the most cautious proponents of change, is the suspicion that all who advocate it, no matter how moderate in scope, vibrate sympathetically on some remote wave length with those who dare to rock the boat. To paraphrase Goffman, "Most of us are glad to see the solid buildings of the world shaken just a little, and though we ourselves may be reluctant to add to the tremors, we feel a grudging sense of respect and admiration for those who do and for the makers of trouble." Mark Rudd and the SDS may be outcasts to most of the young and Ashbury Heights may be off limits also to all but a few, but David Eisenhower is out of step with almost everyone.

Whoever writes a book about "The New Humanism," by implication asserts its existence. Whether or not the ideas referred to here collectively as "The New Humanism" really had or still have an existence outside of the mind of the author, is something I do not wish to be pressed about. To paraphrase Berkeley, "Esse est percipii." Ideas have a rather strange existence of their own, quite independent of the realities thy represent — a discovery first advanced by Plato and argued by philosophers ever since. Possibly some ideas, like self-fulfilling prophesies, may gain reality just because some people write about them as if they did exist. Thus, a new philosophy of life may attract more and more people simply because somebody is taking it seriously enough to write about it. The very books

10

that described, explained and analyzed the so-called "new culture" were also most instrumental in creating the very phenomena they were explaining. Consciousness III was experienced by many people only after Reich in his "Greening of America" had focused attention on its rather shadowy existence. In fact, it gained much of its reality only *after* Reich postulated its existence.

Ideas also have a past and to quote Heraklitos, "Nothing is quite new under the sun." Humanism in any form is anchored more firmly to the past than any other ideology. The new humanism is no exception. Its roots are anchored in science as well as religion, both of which have a respectable past and both have nourished the better instincts of man.

The ideas assembled between the pages of this book are admittedly half-baked. They are set adrift in hopes to provoke the reader to come up with better and more precise ones. They are not to be judged as finished products, but rather as an invitation to all who have thought about the same or similar issues, to reply, to refute, to sharpen and to expand the arguments presented here. If better, sharper, more focused and more precisely formulated ideas emerge to supersede those expressed here — fine!

Having been trained in the ways of science where every interpretation of observable facts must constantly parry with the minds of others thinking about similar problems, I strongly believe that no man can see the whole truth but only a very restricted part of it. Each man, so to speak, is a monad. This author prefers to act like one of Leibniz's monads, which mirrors the universe in its own highly restricted individualistic way. The New Humanism, like any cultural phenomenon, will only be understood in its entirety after it has been mirrored by many different monads.

For openers, I offer my own mind as a lens through which the ideas, hopes and aspirations that excited so many members of the generation that grew up during the 1960's and early 1970's and a more restricted number of the generation that grew old during that decade, can be focused, bent and reflected. Using an imperfect lens, the images that it projects will be blurred and unequally focused, but any lens, no matter how restricted its revolving power, is better than no lens at all.

If I WERE TO WRITE my own review, I would start off like this:

> " 'The New Humanism' is not an elegant book. Its chapters are loosely strung together, laden with often unfocused eruditions; it lacks theoretical drive, and its argument is repetitive — not all of it is consistent. The writer's prose is cumbersome — although, fortunately, not obscure — and the text is labored, even dutiful, as if a lesson had to be gotten through. But I suppose it has some socially redeeming value."

The Origin of the Arousal

I

To inquire into the reason for the so-called "youth revolt" or alienation of the young is really a double barreled undertaking. Youth revolt is probably a natural phenomenon and part of the human condition of all societies past, present and future. The identification of all the constellations of different pressures existing in any given country at any given time that would enable one to predict the sparking of a youth revolt, could well be an attractive project for qualified historians, but is obviously beyond the scope and certainly beyond the qualifications of this writer. But it may be relevant to point out that "youth rebellion" and "generational conflict" of the kind encountered for the first time in America during the last decade have had their parallel in European societies of earlier ages and have in fact been an integral part of modern European history at least of the 19th and 20th centuries.

One is almost a bit embarrassed about using terms like "youth rebellion" or "alienation," or "generation gap," for fear that they have been flogged to death by countless magazine articles and paper books so that by now these terms have become clichés rather than concepts. The trouble with clichés, of course, is most of them become just that precisely because they are so true, or at least because they denote a strong element of truth.

Our exaggerated vocabulary stimulates an imagery of a whole generation of young either declaring war on their parents and teachers or turning their backs on them in contempt, or of a gulf of misunderstanding separating the three generations (remember grandparents are alive now too since longevity has been extended).

Nothing is probably farther from the experience of most ordinary Americans who get along reasonably well with their children except when they turn on their record player too loud. Walter Laqueur in his book, "Out of the Ruins of Europe," devotes a chapter on "Reflections on the youth movement" and points out how most of the basic beliefs and outward fashions of the present world youth movement merely illustrate the point that history repeats itself and that nothing completely new ever happens.

> "Most of the basic beliefs and even the outward fashions of the present world youth movements can be traced back to the period in Europe just before and after the First World War. The German Neue Schar of 1919 were the original hippies. Long-haired, sandaled, unwashed, they castigated urban civilization, read Hermann Hesse and Indian philosophy, practiced free love, and distributed in their meetings thousands of asters and chrysanthemums. They danced, sang to the music of the guitar, and attended lectures on the 'Revolution of the Soul.' The modern happening was born in 1910 in Trieste, Parma, Milan, and other Italian cities where the Futurists arranged public meetings to recite their poems, read their manifestoes, and exhibit their ultra-modern paintings. No one over thirty, they demanded, should in future be active in politics. The public participated actively at these gatherings, shouting, joking, and showering the performers with rotten eggs. In other places, things were not so harmless. 'Motiveless terror' formed part of the program of a group of young Russian anarchists, the Bezmotivniki, in their general struggle against society. The Bezmotivniki threatened to burn down whole cities, and their news sheet featured diagrams for the production of home-made

bombs. Drug-taking as a social phenomenon, touted as a way of gaining new experience and a heightened sensibility, can be traced back to 19th-century France and Britain. The idea of a specific youth culture was first developed in 1913-14 by the German educator Gustav Wyneken and a young man named Walter Benjamin who attained literary fame. In 1915, Friedrich Bauermeister, an otherwise unknown member of the youth movement, developed the idea of the 'class struggle of youth.' Bauermeister regarded the working class and the socialist movement (including Marx and Engels) as 'eudaimonistic'; socialists, he admitted, stood for a just order and high living standards, but he feared that once their goals were achieved they would part ways with the youth movement. Bauermeister questioned whether even the social revolution could create a better type of man, or release human beings from the 'bourgeois and proletarian distortions.'

"The ideas of this circle were developed in a little magazine called Der Anfang in 1913-14. Youth, the argument ran (in anticipation of Professor Kenneth Keniston), is not yet integrated into society. Unencumbered by the ties of family or professional careers, young people were freer than other elements of society. As for their lack of experience, for which they were constantly criticized by their elders, this, far from being a drawback, was in fact a great advantage. Walter Benjamin called experience the 'mask of the adult.' For what did the adult wish, above all, to prove? That he, too, had once been young, had disbelieved his parents, and had harbored revolutionary thoughts. Life, however, had taught that adult that his parents had been right after all, and now he in turn smiled condescending superiority and said to the younger generation: This will be your fate too.

"For the historian of ideas, the back issues of the perio-
dicals of the youth movement, turned yellow with age,
make fascinating reading. The great favorites of 1913
were Hermann Hesse, Spengler's Decline of the West,
Buddhism and Siddhartha, Tagore's gospel of spiritual
unity (Love not Power), and Lenin. It is indeed un-
canny how, despite all the historical differences, the
German movement pre-empted so many of the issues
agitating the American movement of today, as well as
its literary fashions."[1]

It is interesting that so little has been recorded of the
impact youth movements have made on the History of Ideas.
Possibly the reason for the paucity of information on this subject is not just an oversight by historians but perhaps because
most of the impact that was made by youth movements was
on social action rather than in the area of ideas and ideology.
In the past, youth movements signified little more than resistance "to growing up" because growing up meant exchanging
friendships and camaraderie for commercial relations, and close-
ness to nature for the treadmill imposed by office and job to
the altar of success. But since growing up was inevitable, such
poetic emotions could hardly make much of a lasting impact.
    In Germany, the "Wandervoegel" and the "Kameraden," in
England and France the Scouts, and their counterparts in other
countries might be fondly remembered like "Paradise Lost"
by those who once walked with them but had now outgrown
them. Since in the end one had to grow up, however reluctantly,
there was ultimately nothing left to do but to exchange knee
pants and all the other paraphernalia of "youth" and to conform to the ways of the hated bourgeois.

"The early history of the Wandervoegel is that of a
group of high school students who went hiking through

---

1. From Walter Laqueur's "Out of the Ruins of Europe," The Library
Press, New York, 1971.

the German countryside unaccompanied by adults. But hiking and the rediscovery of nature were not the main purpose of the movement, which quickly spread throughout Germany. One went on such excursions to escape the control of teachers and parents, to experience the togetherness, the new Lebensgefuhl. This emerged even more clearly during the second phase of the youth movement, when the ideologists took over. A study of the literature of the period involves reading a great many romantic effusions, a great deal of nationalist bombast and plain gibberish — an undertaking liable to tax the patience of even hardened students of history. But it is nevertheless a worthwhile effort, likely to provide food for thought for a whole generation of historians, sociologists, and psychologists with an interest in youth revolt. The German youth movement experienced most of the problems and expressed almost all the ideas which continue to preoccupy students of generational conflict to this day. For this reason the study of the movement cannot be recommended warmly enough."[2]

Of more consequence were those youth movements that aimed at more than just trying to be young but who allied themselves with a section of the adult world; usually the one not in command. The ideals that turned youth on were rarely if ever articulated by one of their own. The heroes of European youth were Hermann Hesse, Romain Rolland, Martin Buber, Rainer Maria Rilke, Stephen George, Oswald Spengler, Tagore, D'Annuzio, and of course Marx, Engel, Lenin, Herzl, just to name a few; and I apologize for adding in the same sequence to the list the names of Hitler, Mussolini and Stalin, but they were, unfortunately, heroes to some of the idealistic as well as the opportunistic among the young.

––––––

2. From Walter Laqueur's "Out of the Ruins of Europe," The Library Press, New York, 1971.

It is one of the more vexing paradoxes of modern history that the three most oppressive social orders that were ever invented, namely, Communism, Fascism and Nazism, managed to promote the illusion that they represented a departure for something new and thus found among the members of youth movements their most enthusiastic allies. Men live by illusion, and Nazis, Fascists and Communists benefited alike by nurturing this illusion. To wit, the fascist anthem starts with an appeal to the young generation, "Giovenezza, giovenezza, primavera di belezza." The more liberal societies of Europe to this day found looking young to be more difficult.

> "Youth movements have always been extreme, emotional, and enthusiastic; they have never been moderate or rational (again, no major excursion into the psychology of youth is needed to explain this). Underlying their beliefs has always been a common anti-capitalist, anti-bourgeois denominator, a conviction that the established order is corrupt to the bones and beyond redemption by parliamentary means of reform. The ideologies of democracy and liberalism have always been seen as an irretrievable part of the whole rotten system; all politicians, of course, are crooks. Equally common to all youth groups is a profound pessimism about the future of present-day culture and an assumption that traditional enlightened concepts like tolerance are out of date. The older generation has landed the world in a mess and a radical new beginning, a revolution, is needed. Youth movements have never been willing to accept the lessons of 'the past'; each generation is always regarded as the first (and the last) in history. And the young have always found admiring adults to confirm them in their beliefs."[3]

-----

3. From Walter Laquer's "Out of Ruins of Europe," The Library Press, New York 1971.

Youth movements, however, invariably start out apolitical or at least initially are fed by emotions, aspirations and hopes which transcend political objectives. Protests against lack of vitality and warmth and pity, against egotism, snobbery, selfishness, hypocrisy, and hope for revival of sincerity, decency, open-mindedness, brotherhood, love, truth and beauty are the raw materials of youth movements, past and present. Whoever describes a youth movement as idealistic only states the obvious. Youth movements, as Laqueur pointed out, have never been out for personal gain. What motivates them is different from what motivates an association of manufacturers. The bond created by an association of young people provides to its members a depth of emotional experience, which no association of elders can match, even though their aims may be much better articulated. Unfortunately, the intensity of that experience is inversely proportional to its longevity. I know of no instance where the "humanism of youth" or their longing for the "good life" which fired them at 14, and 18 was ever translated into a life style that could be continued when one reached the age of 25 or 30; unless it was joined to a program for revolutionary action. But such programs were articulated usually by their elders. The only possible exception that comes to mind are the "Kibbutzim" established in Israel prior to the establishment of the Jewish state. The great attraction they held even for the non-zionist youth of Jews and lately even some young guilt-ridden German youths was probably because the Kibbutz offered a way of life where the "I and Thou" relationship of Martin Buber, which fascinated the young Jews of the Buende in Central Europe could be continued forever unthreatened by the commercialism of the outside world. But even the Kibbutzim, I suspect, succeeded only because ultimately they became a very useful and efficient organization that met both the unique economic and defense needs of the rather unconventional State of Israel.

One of the very few places untouched by the cult of youth was America, itself a young country, unencumbered by the dead weight of tradition: "Amerika," Goethe apostrophized, "du hast es besser . . ."

II

It has been said of youth movements, "blessed is the land that has no need of them." America for a long time was such a land. It alone among major Western countries did not experience generational conflict.

> "For one thing, the burden of the past was not felt as heavily in America as it was in Europe. Less distance separated parents and children, teachers and students; adventurous young men went West, the country was forever expanding; society as a whole was far less rigid. Then in the 20th century, when these factors had ceased to be quite so important, America was spared a movement of youth revolt by a series of economic and foreign political crises."[4]

Other reasons, some of them perhaps more important than those enumerated by Laqueur come to mind that may have contributed to the circumstance that in America for a long time the distance that separated children from their parents, teachers, superiors and government was so much smaller than in other lands. Let us remember that the mood and the tone, the style, the orientation and Weltanschaung in this country is largely set by the members of the middle class, or at least that articulate minority of the middle class that acts as spokesman for the rest of us. The very rich really form an island for themselves, who in their yachts and country houses are

---

4. From Walter Laqueur's "Out of the Ruins of Europe," The Library Press, New York, 1971.

culturally as far removed from the rest of us, as are the monks of a Buddhist sect. The very poor are much too busy making ends meet to contribute to "ideology." When, as during the 60's, they made sufficient noise to awaken the rest of us, ideas such as those advanced by the civil rights movements really made not much impact until the middle class sons and daughters (both black and white) adopted these thoughts and went out to do battle for them. Until recently, however, large numbers of middle class boys and girls were offspring of immigrants and as such their natural inclination to set themselves apart from their elders was directed toward losing the foreign accent of their parents and shedding the heritage of their Irish, Jewish, Italian, Russian, or Polish ancestry, which might restrain them from fully assimilating and swimming in the mainstream of life in America. For them the new future was right here and to sail into it required a kind of private rebellion. So, in America, the so-called generational conflict was blunted and remained strictly an intra-family squabble. The native sons and daughters were just as eager to conform probably because their buddies with the foreign-sounding, unpronounceable names had convinced them that America was really young, wild, clever, progressive, dynamic and future-oriented and free of all the nonsense and pretensions of their European ancestors.

In Europe before World War II, young people would wear kneepants until they were 20 as a sign that they belonged to the elite of youth. In a sense in America we all wore "kneepants." We dressed and acted, spoke and felt "young." John Lucas expressed similar sentiments.

> "I question the rosy image of America's remembered young people. When I came to this country the young amazed me. Here, unlike Europe, the parents were often liberals; the young were conformists to the bone. They were conformists even — or perhaps especially — when they thought that they were wild. They could be infan-

tile in the worse sense of the word, since the entire American cult of youth was developed to the point of despair. To the short-sighted fools who prattle about how puritan or Victorian American family life was a generation ago, I suggest a look at (most of them are old enough to recall) Mickey Rooney's Andy Hardy movies. By 1971, it is Andy Hardy who has aged beyond belief; his father, the judge, remains as believable as ever."[5]

An American youth movement was bound to occur sooner or later though. Youth revolt is a universal phenomenon and part of the human condition. It is also a rule that while youth movements prosper only against a background of rising affluence, they rarely strike roots in a country that is basically optimistic. Obviously, if youth revolt is part of the human condition and if it is a built-in feature of all modern, highly developed societies, then it is obvious that America during the last few decades must have become more like those European countries where confrontations or the emphasis on differences between the "in" generation and the still "out" generation was part of their history.

If it is true that sooner or later a youth movement had to come, then the corollary to this assertion must also be true, namely, that parallel with the Americanization of Europe, there must have taken place a Europeanization of America. By this I mean all those changes that made conditions in America similar to those countries which during the 19th and 20th centuries nurtured large and popular youth movements.

As our enemies would have it, our joining the ranks of the "imperialists" might have Europeanized us by bringing about profound changes not only in our international behavior but

5. John Lucas, "America May Be in its Last Phase of Adolescence," New York Times Magazine, December 5, 1971.

also in our behavior to one another, particularly toward those among us who dissent, doubt, differ and pursue their own way, no matter how far out it may lead. We had the good fortune of having avoided for so long the passions and the frozen rigidity with which different factions in European societies took to and maintained their battle stations. Oh, we had plenty of conflict, but as long as they were conflicts of interest rather than battles between true believers and heretics, the whole struggle had a young look. Interests have a way of shifting, and yesterday's opponents can emerge as tomorrow's allies as long as they fight for each other's possessions rather than each other's souls. In Maine and New Hampshire, even the village communist (synonymous with village idiot or Democrat) shared in the nightly card game or the Sunday barbecue as long as he trimmed his hair, washed his neck and wore a clean shirt.

"In this country accepted ideas are institutions. In almost every instance during the last 25 years where America has changed for the worse it has happened because of increasing extreme application of what seemed to be new, but what were, in reality, old and corroding ideas. When I came to the United States I met a society whose dominant ideas included the desirability of world democracy, progressive education, global communication — in sum, of the endless improvability of society, achievable through large material expenditure and a measure of good will. (Note that I write 'the improvability of society.' It took me a quarter of a century to recognize that both the standard American assertion and the standard European conservative criticism of the American Idea missed, and misses, its essential thrust. From the very beginning, Americans have been concentrating not so much on the improvement of man as on the improvement of society — two aims that are, of course, different and even contradictory on occasion.)"[6]

Lucas' statement implies in more elegant language that those who are engaged in the improvement of men rather than his institutions, in the past invariably have made up their minds that if they cannot save souls, it is better to kill the bodies wherein reside the souls who are resisting redemption. This general predisposition has not really come to rest in Europe with the end of the Middle Ages as is generally believed but is very much in vogue among people involved with the dissemination of ideas. In the Europe before and between the wars, Royalists, Republicans, Clericalists, Stalinists, Trotskyists, Socialists and Communists argued ferociously with one another more often on the streets than in the debating halls. Coexistence was practiced only on the playground among the children of different parents who were often not on speaking terms with one another. No wonder that when the same children grew up to be sensitive adolescents, they resisted giving up the old camaraderie and held up "youth" not just as a stage of development, but as a way of life never to be abandoned. The parallel to the conditions that had existed in faraway lands during the earlier part of the 20th century and those that emerged in our own midst after 1960 is obvious.

Unlike in Europe, politics used to be a sport here. *We* used to take pot shots at the President; *Europeans* paid homage to their sovereign. There were no villains *here*, only jerks. When McCarthy accused Truman and the "Democrat" Party of treason, he was as much out of step as the cartoons depicting American history as conspiracies hatched by "Merchants of death" or "Wall Street Bankers." Neither version convinced nor aroused anybody who lived on Main Street, U.S.A. The Europeanization of America signaled for us not so much a

-----

6. John Lucas, "America May Be in its Last Phase of Adolescence," New York Times Magazine, December 5, 1971.

change in our basic beliefs and convictions, but merely amplified the zeal with which we now hold these truths not only self-evident, but also sacrosanct. In this process of transformation, we have lost both our sense of humor and irreverence, the two main features of youthfulness. By irreverence I mean the unerring sense of precision which Americans have perfected to recognize the gasbags among them and the accuracy with which they could plunge the needle into the proper site to let out the gas that reduced the pompous down to their proper size.

Our heroes were Bogart and Chaplin. The extent to which we repudiated them and the enthusiasm by which they have been rediscovered by a new generation measures the gap in taste betwen the young and middle-aged.

America, in the 60's, so Laqueur tells us, was a prosperous country, but it was no longer optimistic; the American dream had been lost on the way to affluence. It seems, of course, rather strange that the loss of optimism should have occurred precisely in a generation that was marching double time toward affluence, full employment, two cars in every garage and two bathrooms in every house. But, on second thought, optimism always blossoms best in hard times, maybe because optimism is the necessary ingredient for survival.

Failure and deprivation are much harder to take when the distance that separates us from the attainment of our goal is still large and difficult to negotiate, than when the promised rewards are only inches away, but still out of reach. The frustration then becomes tantalizing. In a jet plane arriving three hours later than scheduled on a transatlantic flight to London tempers will start burning, while a passenger on an ocean liner may hardly notice when his ship arrives at destination one whole day late. Every college kid who rubbed elbows only for a year with science or social studies, even if he forgot all the formulas he had crammed, had imprinted upon his mind the certainty that to modern man as of now are available all the tools that can eliminate most of the causes of human misery and poverty that have operated to deprive and threaten man since the beginning of time. Cures for the eradication and disposal of sickness, disease, hunger, poverty, slavery, back-breaking toil, prejudice, superstition are available; the only thing that is missing is a willingness and courage to apply them. That was the one take-home lesson which almost every college freshman remembered and that is why the impatience started and spread from the campuses, for when they looked out at the real world, they found their parents and the government which their parents had voted into power still playing the identical games that fascinated Metternich almost 170 years ago. In America, the most trusted presidential advisor on national security spent the first part of his life studying Metternich's every thought and the second part of his life imitating his actions, both of which seemed to them unworthy of imitation.

It is, of course, no accident that so much of the turbulence, both intellectual and emotional, should have originated on the campus. The dissent of the young could not have been possible had it not been nourished by the tradition of free inquiry which is the very lifeblood of the university itself. Like the ghosts whom the sorcerer's apprentice invoked, the dissent that sparked the campus unrest was perhaps more than what the universities had bargained for. The unfortunate "truth" is that this generation for the first time has taken seriously some of the insights that university scholars have revealed about our institutions and our history. If you were a college kid and had spent so many of your waking hours reading the great books, deciphering the message of ancient religions, reviving the old arguments of classic, neoclassic and modern philosophy, you were more likely to perceive the not-so-subtle difference between the ideals you were taught to uphold and the practices by which the world operated.

Historically, all of this would have been just as irrelevant as other earlier foreign youth rebellions if the home-grown product of rebellion had not elicited such angry and startled responses by those against whom it was directed. Youth movements as was pointed out before, have come and gone in other countries, and most of them have not been taken seriously. Previous generations of adults, who were more certain of their tradition and values, less ridden by feelings of guilt, have shown less concern with the rebellions of their sons and daughters. The middle-aged, middle-class parents of today clearly did not feel themselves to be in any such position of certainty. They were either, therefore, profoundly disconcerned by the onslaught of the young or, if they were intellectuals, or liberals, they were within limits sympathetic with the idealism of their offspring — particularly if intellectually they did not stray too far from the middle of the road which they had taught them to walk. We, the adults, after all, applauded their participation in the civil rights marches or their joining the Peace Corps or VISTA. We may have objected to their bad manners or over-zealous shouting, but few of us will deny even today that if the peace marchers had not shouted so loud or if they had matched our good manners with the same acquiescence to the war and to those who perpetrated it, as we, their elders did, the war in Vietnam might still be on. Along with the annoyance at the arrogance and "holier than thou" attitudes with which so many students continuously instructed us on all our sins and congenital social defects, we probably experienced the uncomfortable feeling of guilt for not having manned the barricades ourselves.

There was really no need for us, their elders, to feel so guilty and little cause for the young to feel so heroic. There is "a time and place for everything." Jesus of Nazareth probably knew what he was talking about when he bade his disciples to leave their families and follow him. He probably anticipated that he could not build his church with a band of apostles whose mortgage payments soon became due or whose children were in need of braces.

III

The American youth movement then was prepared by many slow changes referred to as the "Europeanization of America," and probably by many more that escape this onlooker, but it was sparked off by the most traumatic event of our time that shattered all our illusions about ourselves, *The War in Vietnam.*

The preamble to Jean Francois Revel's best selling book, "Without Marx or Jesus," starts like this:

> "The revolution of the 20th century will take place in the United States. It is only there that it can happen. And it has already begun. Whether or not that revolution spreads to the rest of the world depends on whether or not it succeeds first in America."[7]

Americans may feel bewildered, skeptical, glad or sorry to hear the news; but most of them will not believe it. Eventually, disbelief will give way to assent if one rewrites the Frenchman's curious statement to read that perhaps "Americans have glimpsed the future by having come into possession of unlimited power, only to be dragged subsequently into an unconventional 'conventional' war against one of the humblest of people. Both situations were unique to the American experience and coping with them has become then American preoccupation, after having come face-to-face with two of the horsemen of the modern apocalypse, unlimited power and limited war."

To paraphrase Reich, the over 40 generation has accepted tax loops for the rich, shoddy goods, police graft, corrupted

---

7. From J. Revel's "Without Marx or Jesus," Doubleday and Company, 1971.

and lying politicians, unsafe cars, poisoned foods, poisonous drugs, built-in obsolescence, death-trap highways, overcrowded prisons, hospitals that do not heal, and all the other ills of our society with a stoicism reserved for natural disasters. The new generation might have accepted all that too, less stoically perhaps, than we did but still they would have found it possible to live their own lives and "do their thing," if only Death, either of the sudden and violent kind through war or the slowly choking kind through pollution, had not been introduced to them as a constant companion. To a generation so much "in love with life" as they were, that companionship turned out to be unpalatable.

"The war seemed just another activity and, indeed, it did not pierce the consciousness of many of the middle class, who continue to accept it as 'necessary,' just as they accept pollution, automobile deaths, or chopping down the redwoods. But the war should not have been offered to our young people. They were the wrong market. And when they began to be killed, their parents were the wrong market too. The war did what almost nothing else could have: it forced a major breach in consciousness. . . . It might have been years before marijuana and riots catalyzed disillusionment. The war did that with extraordinary rapidity. It rent the fabric of consciousness so drastically as to make repair almost impossible. And it made a gap in belief so large that through it people could begin to question the other myths of the Corporate State. The whole edifice of the Corporate State is built on tranquilizers and sleeping pills; it should not have done the one thing that might shake the sleeper awake."[8]

-----

8. From C. A. Reich's "The Greening of America," Random House, New York, 1970.

So much has been written about the war that it is almost embarrassing to add one single word to the billions that have been poured out already in print or over the airwaves on this most tragic topic. If it had never happened, there would have been no youth revolt, no generation gap, no counter-culture, no alienation and no book on "The New Humanism." But the Vietnam war is to Americans an issue that looms as large as does the holocaust to the Germans who remember the Nazi intoxication of the past. Though the Vietnam war is not comparable in scope or magnitude with the crimes of the Nazi holocaust, it is one of those collective undertakings which propelled this nation deep into the tangled and difficult twilight zone of national morality and collective versus individual guilt, and the young would not let us forget it.

"The anguish and rancor provoked by the Vietnam experience overwhelm everything else at the moment for those who reached the age of military service during the last ten years. Every parent of a boy in this age group knows the impact of this experience. Being asked to risk one's own life and to kill others in a war which has never engaged official or popular enthusiasm is hard to accept. When to that is added a rising crescendo of popular opposition and an ever-widening concern about the constitutionality of the war, the candor of its spokesmen and the morality of its conduct, the anguish is sharpened. When this had to be faced in the context of a Selective Service law visibly inequitable in its inconsistent and occasionally abusive administration, it became a prescription for torment and resentment. Because of the student deferment, the campus became a purgatorial sanctuary for four years of intense argument in which the cynical evader sparred with the conscientious objector and the dutiful draftee. This experience was bound to make a deep and permanent imprint on the outlook of a whole generation."

The question arises why should a single, limited far-away war, which hardly caused a ripple of discomfort among the middle and upper classes of the over-30 generation cause such tremendous revulsion and alienation between the parents and children of America. Wars have happened before and sins have been committed both in war and in peace by all groups without turning a whole nation asunder. But the whole idea of a limited war with the burden shifted to a few, while the majority could continue life as usual, was so diabolical a scheme that it almost succeeded, but in the end it backfired. Had this war, like all previous ones in which America fought, engaged major segments of the American population, had it displaced and interrupted all of our lives or kidnapped all our sons, the outcry would have been either so loud and so universal that the dominoes would have been left toppling, where they should have been falling a long time ago, or we all would have clasped hands and joined a common crusade. But this was to be a guns plus butter war; butter for everybody, guns for our children. The young very early realized that this was to be a children's crusade, organized, planned and concurred in by old men, but executed and paid for exclusively by the young.

Children were supposed to be seen and not heard, but American middle-class children coming right out of the homes of the permissive generation and raised on a diet of John Dewey, Progressivism, Dr. Spock and self-expression, were in the habit of making themselves heard ever since kindergarten. They just refused to shut up and the streets became as noisy as were once their playgrounds. The whole hoax might have worked a little while longer than it actually did if the policy

---

9. From Kingman Brewster, Jr. "On our National Purpose," Foreign Affairs, Vol. 50, No. 3, pages 399-416, 1972.

of shifting the burden to the least articulate groups, to the kids of the poor, the disenfranchised, the blacks, and all those who did not know how to buy parole through college or graduate school, had been quietly continued. In a belated effort to correct that inequity, the harassment of the students became the final and fatal blunder, for students are loud and noisy, precocious, and always ready to advise, condemn, judge and argue.

The cause of equality was to be served by impressing youth into servitude through a random and arbitrary selection process, much in the manner of a natural disaster or sickness that might strike some and pass by others. Toward this objective, a national lottery was invented and a game of Russian roulette was played with the birthdays of our children. Imagine the outcry that would have been provoked from the respectable and propertied citizens ˙ had the government tried to raise money by imposing a 100% income tax on some of our citizens in a similar "selective" manner, while totally exempting others.

The question remains: Why should the demand for military service spark such violent anger on the part of those from whom it was exacted? Military service has always been exacted of boys and young men by nation states during the span of the last 150 years without much protest. The sacrificial offering of the flower of each nation's youth was considered an honor, which few dared to decline, and the exchange of iron crosses, gold stars and purple hearts for the battered and bloodied bodies of their sons was a bargain which widows, mothers and fathers were expected to accept without hesitation. But something in the American experience of 1960-70 was sufficiently different this time so that the whole absurdity of the deadly game was revealed and many of the young saw it in a flash. When America, which until 1939 was the most peace-loving and least military nation of all, turned around and translated all the old Prussian slogans into English, it negected to provide the sweetener that made wars acceptable to most and dulled the pain of killing or being killed. These two ingredients were:

1. Universality
2. The creation of a convincing myth

As pointed out above, universality is indispensable if you want to lead a nation to the slaughterhouse. A burden shared is a burden lightened. Adversity equally distributed can make adversity welcome. Every schoolboy knows that it hurts more to be exempted from a spanking than getting one's share of punishment that is administered to the rest of the gang. The reciprocal is, of course, equally true; to be caught in a net from which too many are allowed to escape is infuriating and demeaning to those who are trapped and makes even the lucky ones who get away, feel guilty.

Equally important are myths: "Remember the Maine," "The Union, One and indivisible," "Verdun," "Germany's place in the Sun," "Non pasaran," "Holy Mother Russia," "Making the World safe for Democracy." Men offered their lives and offered them freely and enthusiastically for these and other less convincing causes.

If only our leaders could have made a convincing case for our efforts in that faraway civil war in Southeast Asia, but the domino story just didn't ring true, and by 1968 there was hardly an inhabitant on a college campus who was not plagued by doubts that the only way to exterminate rats, if rats there were, was to burn the whole house down, flood the cellar, and sink the land on which it stands. If the war in Vietnam was, in fact, as its proponents tried to proclaim, the most altruistic act of a great nation that sought nothing more than to make good on its promise to protect a small ally against a bully aggressor, then the job of selling that simple truth was bungled so badly that it defies belief.

Most of us started out by giving the devil the benefit of

the doubt and assumed that decent motives actually started us on our courses. But how was it possible that the leaders of a nation of salesmen that had become so expert in selling almost anything from soap to deodorant could not convince its 180 million customers who by instinct and inclination were eager to believe that as a nation they are the most generous and least self-seeking on earth, of the nobility of their purpose. Could it be that there were just too many loose ends which nobody in power bothered to tie together or to explain? A war that was fought to preserve the liberty of another nation at a price of more than half its people killed or maimed, and practically all of them made homeless, struck our simple minds like a cure for cancer that radiates away the malignant cells along with the good ones. The men in power were so supremely arrogant that they never bothered to address themselves to these minor and nonvirile hesitations.

The explosion of one myth, like all explosions, turned out to be a chain reaction, for suddenly it dawned on an ever-increasing number of people, some young, and some old, that probably all the causes and reasons for which not only this war but probably over 100 wars have been fought in the last 150 years, were foolish or fraudulent, and that there probably was not a single issue that could not have been settled without the expenditure of a single drop of blood if only everybody would not have been in such a hurry.

"Human aggression and the taste for self-destruction which it conceals, the oversimplification of reality made possible by the idee fixé that one is being persecuted, the psychological relief provided by that oversimplification, and the intellectual sloth which it encourages, all make it easy to mobilize the masses in support of a mission which is as obsessional as it is evanescent — and all the more so since four-fifths of mankind has no source of information other than the state which governs them (or claims to govern them). We should not be surprised, therefore, that since 1945, there has been an armed conflict on the average of every five months. Nor should we be surprised to see specialists in the phenomenon of war emphasize, increasingly, the incredible disproportion which exists between the 'objectives' of wars — even when those objectives are attained, which is rare — and the losses which they entail in every area; or even when we see them emphasizing the discrepancies between the importance of the reasons which justify war, and the insignificance of those same reasons, which becomes so sadly evident, after it is all over."[10]

The moment of truth about the war, if it can be called that, came at different times and different occasions but as an intensely personal event to most of the young and the middle-aged. Invariably, it amounted to nothing more than simply waking up one night with an aching heart and suddenly realizing that countless American boys lie dead in Vietnam and many more are probably maimed for life, and that every month more boys are sentenced to a similar fate by a law that utilizes an obscene lottery system to pick its victims for "selective servitude."

In my own case, it was the Cambodian invasion that crystalized my anxious doubts, for it signaled to me a dangerous and frightening turn more foreboding in its possible consequences than the almost mild-manered "Gulf of Tonkin" resolution for which the bill was being paid in weekly installments of dead Americans over a period of seven years. As I look back now, I must admit with a sense of shame that I, along with so many of my middle-aged and middle-class colleagues, could enjoy for so long the cozy war of 1964, 1965,

10. From J. Revel's "Without Marx or Jesus," Doubleday and Company, 1971.

1966, 1967, 1968, when 400 Americans were killed every week and 2,000 were wounded. Fortunately for us, but to our ever-lasting shame, neither the ghosts of 40,000 dead Americans nor of millions of dead, burnt, wounded and maimed Vietnamese ever invaded our meetings or cocktail parties, nor interfered with the fun we had at conventions and study trips to Europe during those glorious years of "The Great Society."

How the change in American attitudes toward the war came about is not important for the understanding of how the young came to distrust and suspect the integrity and good faith of the managers of the institutions which they are destined eventually to inherit. What is important is that, right or wrong, justifiably or unjustifiably, the loss of trust not only in the sound judgment of their elders but also in their good faith, colored the relationship between American children and their parents. American children remembered how their parents never missed a PTA meeting, and how they were constantly talking, ar-guing and sacrificing to enrich their lives with worthwhile experiences. They remembered how busy and dedicated their parents were to the task of enlarging their children's horizons with summer camps and gym instruction and scouting. They took time out to act as Den Mothers and Weblo Fathers. They made sure their children's bite was correct to the tune of $1000 for braces and they were first to purchase Salk vaccine. Their subsequent acquiescence to the draft and the war just made no sense. The patriotism of their parents in the name of which they insisted that their children go to war seemed to them an àct of disloyalty of monstrous proportions and reflected a total disregard for their welfare, which only a few years ago they had guarded so carefully and so devotedly. But when a superstate challenged them to defend their off-spring from being kidnapped, they just flunked the test. At the very best, the parental generation could be accused of hypocrisy because the radicalism of many parents varied in-versely and their hawkishness varied directly with the distance by which their own sons were removed from the draft. No other event did so much to fire the self-appraisals and the arousal of the ethical judgments as the unique American experience provided by the war in Vietnam. One wonders why! My guess is that, unlike all previous wars, this one was denuded of all the hypothalamic reinforcements which mobilized men in the past to fight each other with that extra ingredient of hate or fear of the kind usually released even in the most civilized among us by national obsessions.

To earlier generations (pre-1960-1974) victimized by the apocalyptic fever of international hatred, antagonism, fear and suspicion, such insights as were occasionally voiced by conscientious objectors and pacifists would surface only as a "Katzengammer afterthought," barely audible until after the guns were silenced and the dead buried and the maimed safely hidden away. The American experience with this war (Vietnam) was uniquely different in the sense that the hypothalamus was simply not aroused at all this time. When previously mere mention of the Kaiser, the Czar, the Bolshevics, the Bosche, the Japs, Tojo, the Rhine, Holy Mother Russia, Verdun, the Maine, the Fatherland, sufficed to make the hormones flow, they simply failed to flow this time. Instead, the horror show came through loud and clear and in sharp focus for everyone who cared to watch TV.

The one thing that made this war so different from all previous ones was that its futility and sheer idiocy became evident not, as in all previous wars long after the conflict was over, but long before it ended. The adrenalin supply would not pour out. Too many young minds were totally immune to the national alarm reactions that camouflaged the reason and sensibilities of their fathers in similar earlier episodes. To be sure, other generations, including my own, faced that same dilemma 25 years ago. It took all these years and some of Vonnegut's books like "Slaughterhouse 5" to stimulate retrospect reflection, like a much delayed fuse. It is partly to the credit of the young and partly due to their luck that the blinders of man's hysteria failed to block the field of vision of at least a sizeable and articulate fraction of this generation.

The self-perpetuating acceleration into evil into which any war propels us could only be sensed by a nation that was plunged into a conflict with an enemy that it had never learned to hate or to fear and toward which those gut reactions were never mobilized on a personal level. The reason for the failure to respond to the war in Vietnam via the gut will be argued in time to come. In retrospect, the sinking of the Lusitania, the attack on the Maine, the violation of Belgian neutrality, or the provocation prior to Pearl Harbor might have been just as digestible to the American gut as the alleged attack in the Gulf of Tonkin, but guts are fickle and the things that make them contract fall into no clearly discernible pattern.

It is interesting that the Vietnam War, unlike World War II, has brought forth no G. I. songs, no G. I. humor, no funny stories nor books nor movies; there are no counterparts to "See Here Private Hargrove." Bob Hope would not play it for laughs by "Getting Caught in the Draft" again. It is as if the manufacturers of humor or songs or stories were too embarrassed to even mention Vietnam. The Vietnam war was fought by men who could and would not laugh even temporarily at themselves or at the war or the role they played in it. Some men who fought it could only bitterly condemn it and those who condemned it were even more bitterly condemned by those who affirmed it.

A scene from the movie version of I. Shaw's novel, "The Young Lions," comes to mind. It shows Marlon Brando playing the loyal but decent German soldier who is convinced that all the Nazi wrongs can be corrected after victory; he meets his moment of truth when he overhears a telephone conversation in a deserted concentration camp in which the commander apologizes for his failure to carry out the final act of extermination. Staring evil in the face, Brando runs

38

out and in his fury smashes his gun against the tree, rips off the insignia of his uniform and moments before he is killed by an American bullet, deserts the cause in which he served so faithfully in spite of his many reservations. In a way the young lions of yesterday like Marlon Brando in the novel of that title, discovered what no generation of Americans could ever bring itself to believe, namely, that "we too can be evil." So, the disagreement with governmental policies, but particularly the war during the last decade, sparked much of the "ethical rethinking" and the preoccupation with the concept of evil of American youth.

The immediate problem that occupied the minds of a very large section of young people during the last decade was what stand to take toward a war so many of them had concluded was morally wrong, cruel, inhuman and just plain sinful and evil. The fact that this problem was the most frequently, most heatedly, and most consistently debated issue on and off the campuses, all over the country, is proof that, doomsday predictions notwithstanding, we are still free and freer than most. The soul-searching in response to this very specific question sparked much of the ethical rethinking and the interest in the concept of evil that occupied many of the best young minds. The "evil" to which reference was made so often by both the young and the not-so-young was not only the evil of intent, but also the evil of plain moral inertia. Nobody, at least nobody who deserves to be taken seriously, claimed that we are or were a nation of storm troopers, but what the young critics insisted on saying to us, was that the *consequences* of one's actions, not their *intent*, determines the nature of evil. Morality, or the insistence on measuring all of our actions — the private as well as collective ones — by the yardstick of ethic and moral law became a new dimension that was introduced into our daily lives by the carriers of the so-called "new culture." More was at stake than just the circumnavigation of a dangerous moral cliff from which one could pluge into a moral abyss.

To save oneself at all costs, Canada or jail was chosen in preference to becoming part of one of the thousand My Lais that was being daily enacted. But beyond this immediate objective there was the task of defining the "good life" itself and how it could be lived in the 1960's and beyond. This generation, while having "grown up absurd," had come to like flowers and music, even love and sex too much, to have much use for the enticements of power, glory, status or unlimited wealth. In keeping with the national character, reflection on morality and ethical judgments was less doctrinaire than perhaps in other countries and focused on the specific problems to which they had to be fitted.

> "American dissent is distinguished from European dissent by the fact that the former is involved in problems which are part of reality. Since the dissenters are certain that they will be able to solve those problems, they do not ignore them. They fight against military service in Vietnam, against racial discrimination, against the destruction of the environment, against the relationship of the universities with the military-industrial complex, against governmental indifference toward the American Indian, against the lack of funds necessary to save the cities. For American youth, dissent does not mean the imaginary transference into its society of irrelevant political scenarios, such as Maoism or Castroism; or, if it does introduce such elements, it does so only in small measure, and without using them as an excuse for ignoring real situations. (Some current idols, such as Che Guevara or Castro, are much less remote from the United States, which has interests in Latin America, than they are from Europe; and it is less gratuitous for American youth to revere them than it is for European youth to do so.)"[11]

---

11. From J. Revel's "Without Marx or Jesus," Doubleday and Company, 1971.

Having grown up in a society where man's worth and achievements are measured by the extent to which he ultimately can enlarge himself through his external belongings, his house, his car, his wealth and to the extent to which he can manipulate others, our children feared nothing more than the prospect that if they followed in our footsteps, their lives should be in danger of having made no difference at all except to themselves. For some, the only exit from this dilemma was to repudiate all those commercial relationships to their fellow men that treat the other human beings merely as a means for a specific and well-defined purpose. Communes offered an exit that satisfied their longing for a warmer camaraderie with their fellow men. Less "absurd" solutions were sought by others who also shared the romantic longing to break out of their moral loneliness or isolation and wished to replace the commercialism of human relations where men use each other for all kinds of legitimate and sometimes not-so-legitimate purposes with something of what Martin Buber calls the "I and Thou" relationship between man and his brother.

"There is a growing number among the young of our day who see their future as a process of being fitted into some scientifically well-constructed program, after the data of their life expectancy and capacities and utilizability has been classified, computerized, and analyzed for conduciveness to the purpose, at the very best, of producing the greatest happiness of the greatest number. This moves them to gloom and fury or despair. They wish to be and do something, and not merely be acted upon. They demand recognition of their dignity as human beings. They do not wish to be reduced to human material, to being counters in a game played by others, even when it is played, at least in part, for the benefit of these counters themselves. A revolt breaks out at all levels.

"The dissidents act out or attack universities, intellectual activities or organized education, because they identify them with this huge and dehumanizing machinery. Whether they know it or not, what they are appealing to is some species of Natural law, or Kantian absolutism, which forbids the treatment of human beings as means to ends, no matter how benevolently this is conceived. Their protests sometimes take rational forms, at other times violently irrational ones, mostly exhibitionistic and often hysterical attempts to defy the ruling powers, to insult them into awareness of the totalitarian effect of such policies, whether intended or unintended (the authentic Marxist component of such protests, the denunciation of exploitation and class rule, is not, as a rule, the dominant note). They protest against the destructive effect to individuals of global planning, for the substitution of figures and curves for the direct perception of actual human beings for whose ostensible good all this is being done, especially of those remote from them whose lives the planners seek to determine, sometimes by exceedingly brutal means hidden from their own sight by the opaque medium of impersonal statistics.

"In industrial or post-industrial societies, the protest is that of individuals or groups whose members do not wish to be dragged along by the chariot wheels of scientific progress, interpreted as the accumulation of material goods and services and of utilitarian arrangements to dispose of them."[12]

Finally, the events of 1968 and those that followed signaled for many the shattering of the great American pretension, by

---

12. From "The Bent Twig," Foreign Affairs, 1972.

which I mean the strong belief held until very recently by most except a small radical fringe, that American democracy had provided the final working model within which to solve the age old dilemma of creating a government endowed with power as well as justice. We all shared the belief that if only we could persuade other nations, particularly the young emerging ones, of copying our prescriptions of electing governments with periodic regularity, the danger of their exchanging one form of tyranny for another would be forever averted.

To create governments that are both powerful and just was the urgent task which all nations faced in order to survive in the dangerous time of this century. Most had succeeded in creating reasonably powerful governments. Some of them were even reasonably efficient, but only we in America and a handful of Western nations had created just governments where power was leashed firmly to the assent of the governed. So we believed.

Democracy, we always admitted, may be inefficient at times, unwise, shortsighted, blind, selfish, and sometimes even brutal, when it imposes the tyranny of the majority, but by its very nature, it has a built-in correction factor which in the end will always come to the rescue. So at least we all believed, but this tenet of our "liberal" faith was being questioned under the impact of the events of the last decade by too many of the young.

The discovery so eloquently stated by Senator Fulbright that "power corrupts and absolute power corrupts absolutely" became an article of faith and a point of intellectual departure. Long before Halberstam's book[13] became a best seller, it was dimly perceived that even the "Best and the Brightest" when

––––––

13. David Halberstam's "The Best and the Brightest," Random House, 1972.

they come into possession of power fall victim to it. So the trust in the old platonic prescription that all will be well if only "the philosophers will be kings" evaporated fast.

To assure the survival of democracy required going back to the drawing board to rediscover new sources of wisdom in that most perfect blueprint for government so far designed for an imperfect world, the American Constitution. It meant adapting its formula to the dangerous world of the last third of the twentieth century.

The suspicion aroused against power per se and against those who possess and command it propelled still others into the opposite direction far away from politics and community affairs seeking a kind of Tibetan mountain retreat where encroachment of the cruel and evil outside world would be held to a minimum.

Lastly, the least sophisticated and probably the most simple-minded and certainly the loudest and most vociferous group just advocated the old revolutionary panacea that had never yet increased freedom by one iota, namely, to shift power from those who have it to those who don't. These loudmouths were helped in getting mistakenly identified as spokesmen for a whole generation not so much because what they advocated made sense to so many but because there was a kind of grudging admiration for the troublemakers of the world and for those who would dare rock the boat. A whole generation became a cheering squad, from the distance to be sure, for assorted rebels, not because they believed in what they said (they barely bothered to find out what they meant), but because they were so noisy, and the men who wielded the power from 1960 to 1970 impressed them as even more of an unsavory lot.

One can forgive power misused by such charmers like the Black Prince or Richard the Lion Hearted; one may overlook the excess of power when it is placed in the hands of benev-

44

olent despots like Frederick II, Alexander the Great, or adventurers like Napoleon, or when wielded by such inspiring rascals like Teddy Roosevelt, Winston Churchill or Clemenceau, or manipulated by father figures like Woodrow Wilson or Franklin D. Roosevelt, but the men who inherited power and occupied the summit during the ten years just past, did not inspire much confidence. The images of Brezhnev and Kosygin, of Lyndon Johnson and Richard Nixon, Pompidou, Husak, Mitchell, Sadat and Nasser looked too much like a cast of con men engaged in unrolling the unimaginative plot of a B movie.

That kinship, however remote, with the "trouble makers" of the world may have been the cause of much of the anger and misunderstanding between the generations. The relentless recital of the sins and failures of the world's democracies, including the world's most permissive democracy, the United States, to which we were so incessantly treated by our young "betters" became at best a little boring and the confessions of sin and self-flagellation a bit embarrassing and annoying to many who otherwise might have lent a more sympathetic ear to the voices advocating change. The type of conversation carried on in America between young and old was probably carried on in a similar manner in other cultures. In Germany, students threw feces through university windows, in America only rocks; which is judged better and which worse depends on the nature of one's preference,

I have a sneaking suspicion that old Soviet revolutionary heroes were as much turned off by their sons fighting against the rigidity of their bureaucratic system while dancing to the tune of American vocalists, as our hardhats were by the spectacle of war protesters raising the banner of the Viet Cong to the tune of "Where have all the flowers gone?" So the myopia of the so-called "outs" was matched by the hard-of-hearing condition of the "ins." What a constellation for dialogue!

45

It was against the background of these events and predicaments that many of the generalizations, aspirations, and hopes for what may constitute "the good life," both for the individual as well as for the community, were formulated on campus. If the formulae were not very exact or articulate, the search was nevertheless intense, and in a strange and intoxicating way filled us with a sense of excitement and discovery.

The New Humanism, a mood, not a program

I

The objection so frequently thrown at the young that it has almost become a cliché is that the young rebels may know what they are against — but they "haven't got the foggiest" of what they are for, and since they have no plan of their own, they can make no legitimate claim to our attention. They reserve to be shrugged off rather than being taken seriously.

"When young people are pressed for a statement of their values, and one asks what they would make the center of a new world, one is often left with picayune or self-revolving items like never stepping on insects or never throwing away anything made of plastic. This is a blatant use of innocence. We look — often in vain — for a serious, responsible confrontation with the real problems: power, organization in national groups, fidelity in personal life.

"One feels that the younger generation gets particular gratification out of simply attacking the establishment as such. Is it a reaction-formation to their own unease at the affluence of their parents and to their own guilt at their dependency on their parents for sustenance? But this is an unnecessary battle, if for no other reason than that the establishment is dying anyway. The present college generation was

born in an era when practically all mooring posts —
i.e., in sex, in marriage, in religion — are threatened or
already lost. We have a new morality, most obviously
in the areas of sex, marriage, and the role of women.
No one can doubt that a new electronic technology
is fast revolutionizing our economic and communication systems. Religious practices are also involved in
profound change, what with ersatz Buddhists, Yogis,
and Hindus springing up on all sides. One age is dead
and the other not yet born — ours, which includes both
youth and age, is in limbo."[1]

Those who say that the young people know so well what
they are against but know not what they are for are, of
course, absolutely right, but that is not a new dilemma. The
answer to what ought to be is always much harder to come
by than the answer to what ought not to be. As long as we
are not prepared to give up that old American prejudice that
through history there runs a thread toward progress, no
matter how tangled, the search for the good society is likely
to go on. The City of God will never be found by those who
insist that we already live in the best of all possible worlds.

"We know how difficult it is for dissenters to describe
the kind of society they long for. This lack of precise
ideas, it is sometimes said, is justifiable; after all, it
is up to adults to supply solutions. The role of the
young is merely to express dissatisfaction, modo grosso.
This explanation, however, ignores two facts.   First,
that the spirit of dissent is far from being the exclusive property of the young; and second, that the
spirit of dissent excludes all concrete solutions, for

_____

1. From Rollo May's "Power and Innocence," Norton and Co., 1972.

48

solutions are always partial and always subject to expiration, either short-term or long-term.

"Any technical discussions, any reservations concerning details — even on the part of those who approve of the dissenters' demands, but who emphasize the difficulties inherent in their practical realization — is regarded by the dissenter as an over-all rejection, and as an act of hostility. To begin a technical discussion is to call the dissenter back to reality; and that is something intolerable to someone for whom only total and instantaneous gratification exists, and who therefore cannot accept either the quid pro quo or the step-by-step progress of revolutionary action — let alone of reformism. Everything that contradicts the magical power of words is experienced as a repetition of the original narcissistic wound which was inflicted upon the infant when he first discovered his lack of independence with respect to this environment.

"In this universe of all or nothing, of black and white, there is no question of action, but only of redemption. It is not by chance that dissent has been absorbed into some major branches of Christianity and then refurbished and translated into religious terms."[2]

The New Humanism is not a program; it is a mood that emerged from a deep-felt revulsion against man's inhumanity to man, which is considered the only lasting by-product of all the blueprints and designs that were ever drawn up to insure the betterment of man. To the humanist, the price in human suffering that has been exacted to insure even the most noble 20th century objective has been so staggering that

---

2. From J. F. Revel's "Without Marx or Jesus; the New American Revolution Has Begun," Doubleday, 1971.

he will not willingly approve any further expenditure for its attainment.

The mood was changing, and change in this day and age was not slow. Slogans like "Give me liberty or give me death," "Better dead than red," don't cut much ice any more. The quote, "Ask not what your country can do for you —ask what you can do for your country," did not entice this generation of Americans as much as it did ours only fourteen years ago when these words were first spoken. This famous quotation strikes many of us now as nothing more than a sophisticated retape of "For God, Kaiser and Fatherland" which sent millions to their death twice in half a century and provoked torrents of tears and anguish but in the end failed to add one single ounce of happiness to the life of a single individual.

No one can deny the idealism of patriotic devotion or the virtues of discipline, fortitude, sense of duty, self-denial, honor and integrity which nourished these enterprises, but these virtues are somewhat frozen ones. They tend to arrest and cripple what many now consider to be the highest virtues of man, namely, compassion, tolerance, empathy and justice. The new mood was essentially one of fundamental disillusionment with all doctrines and programs, blueprints and ideologies that call for the sacrifice of life. Having discovered the rhythm of life and the beauty of flowers, the young have begun to wonder whether freedom is really separable from life and whether it can ever blossom on a soil drenched with blood, even of blood shed in its defense. Life is too precious a gift to be bartered away for any man-made abstractions but those that can stand the test, that they will indeed promote more life and richer life. The young generation has finally turned the axiom around and proclaimed, "Life is the most precious gift!" Life is not for sacrifice on any altar but is to be used "to do one's own thing," a sentiment that has been expressed fifty years ago in slightly more eloquent terms by a German-Swiss romantic poet, Hermann Hesse, who in his lifetime, would probably have been voted the most unlikely author to sell a single translatable edition of his work in pragmatic-minded America. He has become the most popular writer of the young. I think I know why! All the heroes of his novels repeat the same agonizing outcry: "Ich wollte ja nur das leben was aus mir heraus wollte warum war das so schwer?" Properly translated, this means, "I only wanted to live what was within me — why was that so difficult?" The translation into 1970 lingo is obvious. The insistence on doing one's own thing so loudly proclaimed by the new generation is refreshing, sometimes startling, but obviously *not* unprecedented. Similar sentiments have been expressed far more eloquently prior to 1960. Reference is made to the literary work of Voltaire, Emerson, Thoreau, Jefferson, Nietzsche, Hesse and Buber. The spirit of life affirmation was no more touchingly described than in C. Reich's "The Greening of America."

"Consciousness III postulates the absolute worth of every human being — every self. Consciousness III does not believe in the antagonistic or competitive doctrine of life. Competition, within the limits of a sport like tennis or swimming, is accepted for its own pleasure, although even as athletes III's are far less competitive (and sometimes, but not always, poorer athletes as a result). But III's do not compete 'in real life.' They do not measure others, they do not see others as something to struggle against. People are brothers, the world is ample for all. In consequence, one never hears the disparagements, the snickers, the judgments that are so common among I's and II's. A boy who was odd in some way used to suffer derision all through his school days. Today there would be no persecution; one might even hear one boy speak, with affection, of 'my freaky friend.' Instead of insisting that everyone be measured by given standards, the new generation values what is unique and different in each self; there is no pressure that anyone be an athlete unless he wants to; a harpsichord player is accepted on equal terms. No one judges anyone else. This is a second commandment.

"Consciousness III rejects the whole concept of excellence and comparative merit that is so central to Consciousness II. III refuses to evaluate people by general standards, it refuses to classify people, or analyze them. Each person has his own individuality, not to be compared to that of anyone else. Someone may be a brilliant thinker, but he is not 'better' at thinking than anyone else, he simply possesses his own excellence. A person who thinks very poorly is still excellent in his own way. Therefore people are in no hurry to find out another person's background, schools, achievements, as a means of knowing him; they regard all of that as secondary, preferring to know him unadorned. Because there are no governing standards, no one is rejected. Everyone is entitled to pride in himself, and no one should act in a way that is servile, or feel inferior, or allow himself to be treated as if he were inferior.

"It is upon these premises that the Consciousness III idea of community and of personal relationship rests. In place of the world seen as a jungle, with every man for himself (Consciousness I) or the world seen as a meritocracy leading to a great corporate hierarchy of rigidly drawn relations and maneuvers for position (Consciousness II), the world is a community. People all belong to the same family, whether they have met each other or not. It is as simple as that. There are no 'tough guys' among the youth of Consciousness III. Hitchhikers smile at approaching cars, people smile at each other on the street, the human race rediscovers its need for each other. 'I felt lonesome, so I came looking for some people,' a III will say. Something in the makeup and pride of a I or II will keep him from 'confessing' that 'weakness' in quite such an open way. But III does not want to stand head and shoulders above the crowd. III values, more than a judgeship or executive title, the warmth of the 'circle of affection' in which men join hands. In personal relations, the keynote is honesty, and the absence of socially imposed duty. To be dishonest in love, to 'use' another person, is a major crime. A third commandment is: be wholly honest with others, use no other person as a means. It is equally wrong to alter oneself for someone else's sake; by being one's true self one offers others the most; one offers them something honest, genuine, and, more important, something for them to respond to, to be evoked by. A work of art is not valued because it changes itself for each person who views it, it retains its own integrity and thus means something unique and marvelous to those who see it. Being true to oneself is, so Consciousness III says, the best and only way to relate to others. Consciousness III rejects most of what happens between people in our world: manipulation of others, forcing anyone to do anything against his wish, using others for one's own purposes, irony and sarcasm, defensive stand-offishness. III also rejects relationships of authority and subservience. It will neither give commands nor follow them; coercive relations between people are wholly unacceptable. And III also rejects any relationships based wholly on role, relationships limited along strictly impersonal and functional lines. There is no situation in which one is entitled to act impersonally, in a stereotyped fashion, with another human being; the relationship of business man to clerk, passenger to conductor, student to janitor must not be impersonal.

"But to observe duties towards others, after the feelings are gone, is no virtue and may even be a crime. Loyalty is valued but not artificial duty. Thus the new generation looks with suspicion on 'obligations' and contractual relations between people, but it believes that honesty can produce far more genuine relationships than the sterile ones it observes among the older generation. To most people, there is something frightening about the notion that no oath, no law, no premise, no indebtedness holds people together when the feeling is gone. But for the new generation that is merely recognition of the truth about human beings. Moreover, getting rid of what is artificial is essential to make way for what is real, and Consciousness III considers genuine relationships with others, friendship, companionship, love, the human community, to be among the highest values of life."[3]

For centuries each generation has taught the succeeding one that in order to be truly noble, a person must be ready to turn in his life for humanity or any goal that promises universal betterment or the improvement of the human condition. The best of each generation, as if driven by a secret death wish, have indeed willingly exchanged their lives for the "greater glory of God," for "the Fatherland," "the flag," "manifest destiny," "the revolution," "the counter-revolution," "the spread of the gospel," "the conversion of the heathens," "the union, one and indivisible," and lately "the defense of the *free* (?) world in Southeast Asia."

Older men have been more cautious about offering their lives too readily, perhaps because part of the wisdom of growing old is the realization that few of man's ideals are worth

---

3. From C. Reich's "The Greening of America," Random House. New York, 1970.

the expenditure of life. Now, for the first time, the secret death wish that drove so many of us when we were young, was being abandoned by our offspring before they, themselves, became too old. Life, itself, is the highest ideal. No more calls for sacrifice of life and limb were to be honored. Doctrines that do not promote life were unattractive and those that require for their attainment service to the point of self-abandonment were regarded with utmost suspicion. The value of any ideology was to be measured not by the grandeur of their aspirations, but by a new yardstick, namely, how effectively does it promote compassion or decrease suffering among men or contribute to the enrichment of the individual's life.

Sparta, as a way of life with its iron discipline and demands for rigorous obedience, may point the road to survival for a garrison state, but it was rejected in favor of the golden rule of tempering justice with mercy, that was followed in Athens. The repudiation of Sparta in favor of Athens may in the long run be of more lasting consequence than all the other noises that have been made by this generation.

The frank admission that we are weary of blood, sweat and tears and want to be "happy" may have seemed to some a shocking rejection of the virtues that shaped and built this country. The spirit of the pioneers who opened the West, the thrift practiced by the inhabitants of New England, the work ethic of the Protestants, the sacrifices which immigrant Jews, Italians, and Irish invested for the sake of the next generation had this much in common, a willingness to forego immediate rewards for the attainment of more lasting, if delayed benefits. This is indeed the true American tradition. But there is also another tradition equally ingrained and part of the American past according to which the pursuit of happiness along with life and liberty is a natural and inalienable right of the individual. Its inclusion in The Bill of Rights, to be guarded by the Constitution, suddenly looms large as a supreme bit of wisdom rather than an expression of a perverted sense of hedonism that might have afflicted some 18th century enlightenment philosophers. It would indeed be considered little more than hedonism, crass and rampant, if it were not for the insight that "nobility of character" and happiness are not mutually exclusive but that probably "you can't have one without the other."

The preoccupation of Americans with happiness and the elevation of its pursuit as a perfectly respectable goal, has made the Stars and Stripes stand out as a rather friendly flag among the more forbidding symbols of other nations. Here in America, until very recently, it has always been understood that the flag had no life of its own beyond the life of the inhabitants over which it waved. The worship of "blood and soil" never gained much popularity among Americans. Earlier American patriotism was correspondingly less intense and never as hyperthyroid as the national exhibitionism of other European nation states. Love of one's country to Americans was a rather personal affair, like the love one feels for one's mother. One does not go around asserting it; in fact, one is almost embarrassed to admit to it, but it is the most lasting love affair one ever experiences.

Along with the death wish, the young have freed themselves also of the so-called "virility syndrome," a form of neurosis that has plagued most males of my generation. The unisex look may be an exaggeration of taste, but it is no more exaggerated than some previous dictates of fashion, according to which sexual dimorphism, which in most primates and, for that matter, most vertebrate species, is limited to external genitalia, must extend to the total morphology of the human appearance. Modes of dressing or of hairdo may seem trivial as in fact they are, but they are an affirmation of a mood. Parallel with women's lib, men have lately pursued a liberation of their own, the liberation from the masculine mystique.

My generation and the generation of my father and grandfather have lived with the notion that the measure of man's virility can be scored only by such indices as "sexual prowess" and deceitfulness, competitiveness, dominance, aggressiveness, acquisitiveness, and his ever-readiness to fight, conquer and subdue his opponents. This mystique has lately exploded in a burst of laughter. Shoulder-length hair and beatle necklaces merely signify the hysterical proportion of these outbursts, but a sigh of relief was felt by many men that they need no longer be embarrassed just because they lack the killer instinct and the firm grasp for the next fellow's jugular.

For hundreds of years, playing soldier has been advertised as the manliest of sports; first by the Prussians, then by the Bonapartists, and finally by the Pattons and MacArthurs among us until they had every child six to sixty years old believing it. Lately, an unexpected hitch has developed, however. Old soldiers used to fade away and dead soldiers just disappeared, but because of improved medicine, fewer soldiers die, but more just hobble back, blind, maimed, paraplegic, armless, legless, disfigured, with part of their brain and face blown away. Such survivors of the manly sport of war appeared neither very manly, nor very virile, and as heroes they looked so unimpressive that they made the pursuit of glory across the path of booby traps seem no longer enticing to the young men of the last decade regardless of their testosterone output.

Hunting was out — Ecology was in; so were flowers, sports, music and poetry. The search for the qualities that make us human was on. Competition as a way of life held no mystique. It was supplanted by emphasis on collaboration and cooperation. Rugged individualism, if by that is meant a race where everyone is running against everybody else to get there first and gain the mostest, was out too. "Do your own thing" was the new style, but in this process, many young men and women have learned to be rather good and considerate to one another.

There are those who honestly believe that the erosion of the competitive spirit is just another manifestation of the steady decline and weakening of the moral fiber of American strength, both past and present, a trend that makes us soft and sissy and flabby. Hitler made a similar mistake in judgment 35 years ago. He was so sure that the American youth of that day and for that matter the youth of all the democracies, were much too soft and comfortable a generation to be a match for his legions. He had every American general believing him too for a short time. Well, with the exception of John Wayne, who fought all his battles in Hollywood, American youth of my generation, although they never matched John Wayne's fearlessness, gave a pretty good account of themselves.

The new mood was really neither as unprecedented nor as revolutionary as the advocates of the new culture would have liked us to believe. The change of emotional climate is real enough, but it was mainly a change in emphasis and in style, rather than in content. To their elders, the young appear to be rude and in fact they are. To each other, they are actually quite good and considerate. Witness, for example, the popularity of hitchhiking, which could never have become the national sport in America if there were no junior drivers on the road. It is the young in their hot rods who will stop on the road to help the traveler in distress, provided he is one of their own. Hitchhiking may have become so popular among the young because it is an easily repeatable opportunity to extend an act of friendship to a stranger. In the fellowship of the road, the one who thumbs a ride is not diminished or humiliated by asking for a favor while the one who extends the help is not embarrassed by a request which he may not be able to meet. Neither is reward denied him by the anonymity which makes the usual charitable donation so unsatisfactory a way of doing good.

II

Since life itself is threatened and survival in question, all those who shared the new humanist mood were prepared to do battle in at least two or possibly three causes. "Peace," "Ecology" and "Expansion of Participatory Democracy" are the causes that fire them. The reasons are simple and obvious. War requires their personal surrender quite regardless of whether they are pushed into the ranks of victor or vanquished, a distinction which has become totally meaningless to them. More democracy is the only alternative for regaining a measure of control over their own lives and fortunes, and ecology was an overriding issue because obviously the prospect of gasping for the last breath of air on a continent which has become unliveable just about five minutes before a satellite may have been found with duplicate conditions for supporting life elsewhere, is just the ultimate in absurdity. On the ecology front, all the answers for survival can, of course, only be supplied by their elders and among those only from the scientists. The only reasonable thing they, themselves, can do, therefore, is to follow the experts or at best amplify whatever message those who know best offer as a way out of the pollution morass and then to mobilize whatever action is recommended. When it came to the issue of peace or the expansion of democracy, there were no experts who could be trusted. Instead, they offered their own brand of idealism, a conglomeration more hypothalamic in origin than cerebral, but nevertheless deserving of attention.

To promote peace, their voices urged us to try something new and something entirely different, and they pleaded with us to break the vicious cycle of war succeded by short, uneasy peace, followed by more terrible war which, with the periodicity and precision reserved for recurrence of the business cycle, has swallowed the flower of every generation for the last 100 years.

Actually, it is a credit to the ingenuity of the political instincts of Western Man that warfare was discontinuous and interrupted by intervals called peace. The final balancing sheet of victims maimed and killed would probably not have differed much if since the day Napoleon III was defeated in 1871, Europe had continued fighting a 100-year war, instead of interrupting the proceedings with periodic rest periods that only served to retool the participants for greater bursts of ferocity.

For my generation, "collective security" became the article of faith, but this principle simply lacked the power to inspire the many. How could one propel large numbers of people into action on that principle as long as differences were stressed and glorified and the similarities that are shared by a wider humanity remained obscured? France and England as late as 1938 could not really bring their people to fight for the far-away Czechs even though the "bells tolled" loud and clear for them. Americans, or at least a great majority of them, persuaded themselves that they translated "collective security" into action in Korea and Vietnam; and as we all know by now, it did not work.

The irony is that we actually almost succeeded in breaking the vicious cycle. The totality of the World War II victory combined with perhaps the balance of terror has actually prevented major confrontations of the kind engaged in 1914 and 1939. It is 30 years after VE/VJ Day. The clock stands at a greater distance now as it was on Armistice Day, 1918. By the time 30 years that followed the signing of documents in the Forest of Compiegne in 1918 had elapsed, the world was already through another war. Today, VE Day plus 30 years later, the prospects for another big confrontation are fairly dim.

There is logic in the argument of the young that just as the "Balance of Terror" constitutes an entirely new, unprecedented but uniquely successful peace-keeping force that was holding the giants at bay, so new, unprecedented, and totally untraditional methods need to be tried to prevent the more orthodox military disasters from occurring (and every war is a disaster, particularly for those in whose behalf they are being fought and for those who do the fighting).

That old bogeyman, the "Balance of Terror," does not frighten the new generation as much as it did mine. In fact, to an increasing number, it looks like one of the happiest arrangements of the otherwise not-so-happy post-World War II period because it managed to save us not only from collision with our enemies, but it also saved us from ourselves.

There was a time when we all thought that God gave "Man" another chance when he first let the Americans rather than the Germans or Russians or Chinese in on the secret of atomic energy. When the American monopoly ended, many of us sincerely felt that history had taken a new turn for the worse, and that we were so much closer to disaster. The reasons for these sentiments were obvious. As long as the fearful weapon was in the hands of America, the world had little to fear. No ruthless blackmail would be committed and we would never, never drop the bomb except in self-defense. This somewhat prejudiced view of history was obviously not shared by the Russians or Chinese, or, for that matter, not even the people of the so-called Third World. It is also no longer subscribed to by a growing number of thoughtful people, both old and young, in our own country.

To a Toybean view of history, it may well appear that catastrophe was prevented during the last 30 years precisely because atomic energy did not remain anybody's monopoly, not even America's, for very long. The Toybean interpretation of history may conclude that the survival of civilization was indeed initially well served by the circumstance that America, rather than Russia, prevailed in the coldest days of the cold war and that America rather than Nazi Germany won the race for the split atom. Probably there would not have been a stalemate if our competitors had beaten us to the Uranium punch. Few will argue that initially the sole possession of atomic secrets was in better hands with us than it would have been with Russia, China, Japan or Germany, but it is the stalemate itself which subsequently became the guarantor that the big bang-up was not going to happen. It was certainly not our or anybody else's humanity that could be relied upon that resistance to the temptation to use the power of total destruction would prevail indefinitely.

If I were a religious man, I would like to believe that a God who, for reasons only comprehensible to himself, is intent on preserving the human species, would not put too much trust in any of his children's humanity, but would prefer to rely on the kind of stalemate we are having now to serve as guarantor that the total extinction of his stupid children by suicide is not going to happen (at least not yet while he is not sufficiently angry). Of course, it may be argued by his detractors that if such are his intentions, his wisdom may not be as infinite as he is generally given credit for.

In the past, the only alternatives to a world without war were grandiose schemes of "One World," "Union Now," "Federation," "League of Nations," "World Peace Force," or the "Transformation of the United Nations into World Government."

The peace movement of yesterday was seeking a more modest and possibly more realistic slow-motion advance toward universal peace. Instead of supplanting national states, a notion which at the time was obviously absurd because it was so universally unpopular, a revised version of the Oxford Oath was sometimes proposed that called on young men to limit their allegiance to their home states to stop short of war. The Oxford Oath, as probably only the over-50 generation will still remember, was a vow solemnly made at Oxford University by the pacifist-minded students of Britain in 1935 in which they gave notice that they would never participate again in another folly like the one perpetrated by their fathers in the slaughter at the "Somme." Less than five years later, the signers of that oath were filling the ranks of those "few to whom so much was owed by so many."

"The international dimensions of their concern may possibly make the coming generation in the United States and other developed countries therefore not only willing but eager to see the creation of authorities superior to national governments. Those who are in college today after all do expect to be at the peak of their careers when the new century opens. Their children in turn will live most of their lives in the twenty-first century. They are not likely to be satisfied with men tinkering with the present competitive anarchy of sovereign nations."[4]

The peace advocates of today, unlike the pacifists who preceded them, do not apologize for the limitations they, themselves, have imposed on their patriotism which stops at their participation in war. They have partially stepped out of the magic circle of nationalism and allegiance to the state and insisted that national aspirations that require "war" ought not to be implemented at all but ought to be either dropped or postponed until they can be obtained at a less exorbitant price than the one invariably exacted by so-called military action. Most of the so-called "national aspirations," even the most legitimate and deserving ones, are neither so vital nor so relevant to the well-being of the 3½ billion people that inhabit this planet, that they can't wait a few decades for their implementation.

"Today, for example, if we ask what most of the world's three and one-half billion people are doing, it would be true to say: 'Most of them live in Asia, are poor, are ill-fed, are sick, are illiterate, lack freedom, are proud, fear war, and feel neutral in many contests which others think vital. But most people in the world could have been described 'that way a century ago or ten centuries ago. In a sense, the century never belongs to the people who live in it. The City of the

_____
4. From Kingman Brewster's "Reflections on our National Purpose," Foreign Affairs, Vol. 50, #3, pp. 399-415, 1972.

Rich and the City of the Poor was an Aristotelian distinction, not an invention of the hapless Lin Piao.'"[5]

Peace, "the kids" told us, is above all a habit that must be learned just like other good habits, and it is a tradition that must be nourished until we have become so used to it that the alternative to it will have become almost forgotten. Unless we are quite sincere that war or even the threat of war must be ruled out as an instrument of policy, we must be prepared for a long time not to have our way always. It took America 100 years to cultivate a tradition that their union is one and indissoluble. It is conceivable that if we can buy half that time, we can form a similar international habit simply by letting us unlearn war and in the process become so addicted to "peace" that it will be difficult to recondition us into crusading warriors.

Only to Americans in possession of ultimate power and capable of destroying not one country but whole continents in the time span of a few hours, could one seriously recommend as national policy to explore the possibility of promoting and encouraging resistance to war both within one's own borders as well as (far) beyond them in hopes that rebellion could become a serious detriment to any would-be war makers of our own brand as well as of any future foe of ours. That is exactly the prescription we were getting from the more thoughtful of our children.

"In advanced industrialized societies, the goals of military institutions have been subjected to massive criticism and belief in the moral worth of conscript service has been shaken. Hedonism, self-expression, resistance to military authority and a new diffuse moral

_____

5. From Thomas L. Hughes' "Whose Country," Foreign Affairs, Vol. #50, pp. 476-487.

criticism have become paramount among young people. The use of force has traditionally operated within circumscribed limits; new moral and political definitions generate a powerful sense of neutralism and new forms of pacifism. Literary mass consumption and political rhetoric have emerged as more important hallmarks of citizenship than military service. Nationalism itself is muted and mixed with diffuse but powerful feelings of transnationalism. The performance of the United States forces in Southeast Asia, of course, supplied and emotional basis for the emerging popular pacifism. These trends are concentrated among an important minority of young people, but they can be found in various degrees in all parts of the social structure. Thus, in Gerrmany, reluctance to serve in the armed forces and a broad definition of conscientious objection have meant, in recent years, that up to ten per cent of the eligible age groups are exempted from service.

"Comparable trends exist in the Soviet Union and Eastern Europe, but in vastly different cultural settings. Totalitarian control eliminates political and moral debate. However, youth's discontent is widely acknowledged. The Soviet Union has sought to limit the terms of conscripts, emphasized volunteer recruitment wherever possible, and closed important branches of the armed forces to all but volunteer personnel. The military has been downgraded as a locus of citizenship training; this function has been transferred to premilitary personnel assigned for it.

"The Soviet military forces are an integral element of the internal security forces, both at home and in the Warsaw Pact nations. These political realities, plus the validity given to the Chinese threat, mean that personal, moral and even political opposition to military service has no direct or immediate impact on manpower policy, but one should not underestimate the extent to which Soviet authorities are concerned and to which they consider the attitudes of youth."[6]

In one of his evening news broadcasts, Eric Sevareid said recently, "The pacifism of the young would work if only the leaders of the nonfree world could also be persuaded not to fight." To this his young critics responded: It is just possible that the "other" leaders might become convinced or more cautious once we started exporting pacifist sentiments and flood the market with them at a time when the prospective customers seem receptive. Of course, just as one can't export Coca Cola if the exporter shuns the drink, so one can't market pacifism abroad if it is not considered a respectable commodity at home.

It is during the pauses between slaughters when the survivors catch their breaths that "nonviolence" has a chance to be infectious. These intervals are what the German poet, Stefan Zweig, once called "Sternstunden der Menschheit," i.e., light flashes of humanity that can be moments of opportunity used or wasted.

To be viable and convincing, the ideal of "nonviolence" and "conscientious objection" must be so contagious as to become universal. To quote Albert Camus:

"Let us suppose that certain individuals resolved that they will consistently oppose power with the force of example: authority with exhortation; insult with friendly reasoning; trickery with simple honor. They would be preparing for the future. Who can fail to see the positively dazzling realism of such behavior?"

------

6. From Morris Janowitz's "Volunteers, Armed Forces and Military Purposes," Foreign Affairs, Vol. 50, #3, pp. 426-443.

In less prosaic terms, this means, "Suppose they gave a war and nobody came."

Pacifist and non-violent resisters were frequently cornered into an intellectual blind alley when asked such embarrassing questions as, "Would you really sit it out if your home was invaded, your family violated, your freedom usurped, and your way of living dictated by strangers?" or "Would you have refused to take up arms even if it meant letting Hitler take over and deliver you and yours to the gas chamber?" Such questions were really carrying cross-examination too far and besides they missed the essential and unique point conscientious objectors made. Their point was this: When events have propelled us to the point where a choice must be made between these two alternatives, then the cause of nonviolence has already lost and its adherents will probably have to desert it and rightfully so, just as did the students who swore the Oxford Oath in 1935 before they reassembled in the ranks of the RAF. In response to the second inquiries invariably demanded by those who oppose "conscientious objection," their answer was that to demand from a generation born after 1945 that they judge the merits and define their attitude toward a conflict that raged before they were born is as ludicrous as asking the rest of us to clarify in our own minds how we should have behaved in the War of 1812 or whether it would have been proper for us to participate in the Spanish American expedition. I share, of course, with my colleagues and students the conviction that the war of 1939-45 had very different moral dimensions for the fate of humanity than the war of 1812 or the foolishness of "Rough Rider" fame. We also happened to believe that the history of Western man, fortunately perhaps, is by and large *not* a succession of disasters wrought by Attila or Hitler or Stalin but rather a succession of stupid blunders fought over irrelevant issues at the instigation of either fools or bullies or both. It is to these wars that the nonviolent resister addressed himself — not to the earthquakes caused by Attila, Hitler or Stalin.

Those old enough to remember the terrible decade of the 30's have one lesson indelibly inscribed on their minds by the turbulent events of past history when they were "the young lions." That lesson is this: Nonviolent resistance may work with those who operate within the pale of civilized behavior, i.e., Gandhi vis-a-vis the British, but is a totally ineffective weapon against a brutal and unscrupulous enemy who will fill a power void just as surely as nature abhors a vacuum.

Possibly the reason that pacifism never became a credible and convincing ideology among so many of my generation was that our distaste for violence was surpassed only by the deeply held conviction that "turning the other cheek" will not propel us into the City of God but into the abyss. I frankly confess to more than an occasional sense of "reactionary" satisfaction that the presence of American power from time to time has effectively stopped the advance of communist tyranny, when the latter has spread its tentacles. I also believe that if America were to revert to its prewar role of merely exerting "moral force" in an immoral world by acting like a governess scolding unruly nations for their bad behavior and exhorting timid ones to be good by bribing them with candies in the form of foreign loans, then a good portion of the globe will indeed sooner or later, and probably sooner, be faced with the choice of either being *red* or *dead*. On the other hand, the risks involved in the loss of military credibility, if by that is meant the restraint imposed on one's willingness to flex one's muscle, would well be counterbalanced if as the result of the spread of pacifist sentiment the will of other nations to flex their muscles reflexly would in turn also be paralyzed. Only a supremely powerful nation is psychologically equipped to adopt a long-range policy of not always having its own way and in the process gamble away short-range gains for long-range objectives. There is nothing intrinsically catastrophic if a nation, even a great nation, is occasionally thwarted in its ambitions and aspirations. A nation, just like an individual, cannot forever proceed through life without being stopped short occasionally. Failure of gaining objectives does not necessarily imply defeat or humiliation; such defeats, if they can be called that, often turn people inward and teach nations to exchange unrealistic aims for goals more worthy of attainment. For America, in possession of the ultimate power, restraint would hardly by synonymous with defeat or humiliation. More likely, it would be heard as a message loud and clear that our power though unlimited, is guided and controlled by a sense of humanity that imposes restraints on our willingness to use it. The hope that such restraint might start a chain reaction was the young pacifist's creed, and a creed it was — nothing more.

"Agony makes voices shrill. It is hard to tell which is the true signal and which the false. It is like trying to pick out the sound of a bell buoy in a crowded fogbound channel. The danger is that you hear what you want to hear on the one hand, or what you fear on the other. Even a decade of almost continuous conversations with students under circumstances of mutual tension does not leave me with an unambiguous impression. However, I think there are some clear signals.

"First, the oncoming generation does not believe it is either possible or desirable for America to try to keep the peace everywhere in the world, let alone try to impose its own political and economic system on others. This is not just because of limits on our resources. More fundamentally it is a rejection of the pretensiousness of a 'Manifest Destiny' to bring the 'American Way of Life' to the rest of the world. Quite apart from concern about our own troubles, this generation would very much doubt whether our values as well as our institutions would make sense for most other people in contrasting cultures and vastly different states of political maturity and economic development.

"Second, the younger generation is not anywhere near as fearful as their parents were of the prospect of communist world revolution. Dictatorship in proletarian trappings does not seem to them vastly more distasteful than 'dictatorship' in what seems to them feudal form. Their experience — all post-Stalin, it must be remembered — is one of a falling-out among communists. The so-called Red threat has lost its global awesomeness. At the same time they have no illusions about the ruthlessness of the response whenever and wherever dictatorial or imperial regimes are threatened.

"Third, they do worry about the leverage exercised by the military and their industrial suppliers. This I do not think is primarily rooted in Marxism, although some of the old jargon is used occasionally. Their deepest concern is that the power of life and death can be influenced and exercised by private interests and public authorities which are not in fact accountable to those affected.

"Fourth, even if all such interests and pressures were benign and public spirited, the weapons of frightfulness makes the stakes so enormous that the young have a desperate desire for some way by which individual men — particularly the President of the United States and his advisors — can be held in check, lest their fallibility or stubbornness or misguided aim lead them to trip the trigger of nuclear destruction. A generation whose hero-President launched the Bay of Pigs fiasco, and whose mature experience has been dominated by Vietnam misjudgments and by surreptitious wars in Laos and Cambodia, cannot be expected to feel comfortable when the head of the world's strongest power seems to be free to 'go it alone.' President Nixon's insensitivity to this concern led to his terrible misjudgment of what the campus response would be to the style — even more than to the substance — of the Cambodian invasion."[7]

More frightening even than the realization of the ludicrousness and the logical paradox of unwinnable wars was the discovery of the descent into evil toward which war propels those who are forced to fight it, particularly if it lasts long enough and frustrates sufficiently. This, of course, has been primarily a recent American experience and since young Americans were the ones who did the actual fighting, they were the most sensitive to the discovery that even a war fought for such limited national objectives as the Vietnam war, could ensnare us into sins both of commission and omission, as vicious as some of those for which we criticized the Nazis so fiercely.

It is perhaps this perception of guilt and the awareness of moral danger that stimulated during the last decade the preoccupation of so many young people with the Nazi syndrome that engulfed the generation of their parents almost thirty years ago. Any traveler across Europe can testify that the young come in droves to Dachau and Buchenwald, to Terecim and to Auschwitz, to Maidenek and to Anne Frank's house to gaze transfixed at the ruins that testify to man's inhumanity to man. From their ranks come the customers who helped propel the films and books on the Nazi past on to the best seller list. Was it their interest in history? That hardly seems likely. Young people are notoriously insensitive to the things that passed before them, and by their own admission history bores them and teaches them nothing that is relevant or useful. Was it just fascination with evil, total, unlimited, unrestrained and supreme? Maybe, but that does not seem the whole story either. I sometimes think that young people suspected one of

---

7. From Kingman Brewster's "Reflections on Our National Purpose," Foreign Affairs, Vol. 50, #3, pp. 399-415, 1972.

the truths of that awful period more clearly than most of us who lived through it, namely, that "The 1000 Year Reich" was not just a fever curve of a rare disease to which an unfortunate nation succumbed, and whose recurrence can surely be prevented if psychoanalysts, sociologists, economists and associated social scientists are permitted to practice preventive medicine, but that it was part of the 20th century human condition. Perhaps the Nazis were right when they proclaimed that they were the wave of the future.

The descent into evil always starts with the loss of imagination. Once that is accomplished, killing Jews or for that matter killing anybody comes easy. For those who believe themselves to be in possession of knowledge of what is desirable do not commit murder, they merely exterminate that which is undesirable.

It is as if because of the fascination of the sons with the sins of their fathers that a long missing page in the human drama of recent history was finally being inserted. To my generation, the holocaust that started in 1933 and ended in 1945 had remained unfinished business. We have never come to grips with it. Oh, we read and explored all the renditions of the horror story and derived a kind of pornographic thrill and embarrassment, but we never really shared in the despair of the victims who went to their death while we watched from a safe distance in a mood of total indifference and boredom. Had we experienced any sense of guilt then, we would all have been in need of psychiatrists after World War II. Instead, what kept analysts so busy and their couches occupied during the post war period was not our grief nor our guilt complex, but mostly our anxiety over the frequency of achieving erection and emission. Ours was not a "beat" generation nor a "lost" one. We were the "discompassionate generation" that got enough antibody to human compassion in those frightful years of 1930 to 1945 to last a lifetime. To a generation not burdened by memories of events that provided the headlines from 1933-1945, reviewing the Nazi past must have been like staring into a mirror or into a looking glass darkly. The evil that was reflected back and that was so frightening to those who were looking, was not that of the brutal, insolent, sadistic, storm trooper who ruled or thought he was about to rule the whole world, but rather of an insomnia-like inertia of the heart, a sort of "Trägheit des Herzens," a paralysis of compassion. It was the look of the same moral lethargy that they could still recognize in the aging faces of the heroes of yesteryear who had defeated the Nazis; or so they thought.

III

That great American pretension that for so long nourished us that the periodic recourse to the ballot box is by itself enough to insure responsiveness of government to the needs and welfare of the governed has given way lately to some doubts and second thoughts whether "American democracy is obsolete." I should hope not.

"The current student generation's misgiving about the universal wisdom and virtue of the American experiment clashes sharply with the self-righteous scorn for the vicissitudes of the foreigner which has always been such a large part of the isolationist tradition. Also, they are more genuinely imbued with an interest in and enthusiasm about people, nations, cultures other than their own than any preceding generation of Americans ever has been. In part because their skepticism has cast them loose from inherited credos — religions, national, social — they tend to put a higher value on human beings as such, with less prejudgment on the basis of familiarity, traditional relationships, common language, appearance or behavior. All of this is fostered by the fantastic ease with which they wander. To many of them nothing is strange."[9]

The certainty that here in America we have found the fool-proof formula that will provide a stable government without a trace of tyranny has given way to some uncomfortable doubts that our form of government, in spite of all the built-in safety factors, may not be so totally immune from whatever ails other more oppressive societies. You can't have an orderly and highly organized society without a government strong enough to maintain it, and you can't have a strong government without creating an elite that wields the power to do so. To create order with freedom is the dilemma which all governments are still trying to resolve. We thought we had solved both problems, but it turned out the dilemma is still with us.

Maybe Senator Fulbright was right. "Power corrupts and absolute power corrupts absolutely." Suddenly it appeared to some of us that those who were wielding the power, like the Jack in the Box, have outwitted the "lid" of checks and balances of which we were so proud, and have found an opening through which to escape its restraint. We have learned that we too can be manipulated for ends totally different from our welfare, just like other people have been before us; and the needs and aspirations of large sections of our population can be ignored. To paraphrase Salvador de Madariages, "While the citizen is still supposed to be for the state, the state is no longer for the citizen."

The old optimism that progress, however slow, is irrevocably tied to democracy has lost some of its vigor during the last decade. We have learned that just because we elect our officials freely, we cannot prevent them subsequently from thwart-

---

9. From Kingman Brewster's "Reflections on Our National Purpose," *Foreign Affairs*, Vol. 50, #3, pp. 399-415, 1972.

ing the will and aspirations of those whom they are supposed to represent and in whose behalf they are delegated to act. By 1970, a large number of young people thought they had made the original discovery that techniques have become available to monarchs, dictators, and parliaments alike that enable them to manipulate minds in such a way that it is indeed possible now "to fool almost all the people all of the time."

Let us not belittle our past accomplishments, however, just because of some present-day failures. What we have done successfully is to distribute power by dividing it by three and to set a limit on the time span during which power can be exercised by any one individual or any group of individuals. This is no mean achievement in itself, particularly when we look around us and face our critics who could not even accomplish this. Once that power has been transferred from the people to those whom they duly elect into authority, however, even if it is done with the widest popular consent, the channels by which the will and aspirations of the people can be made known to those who don't want to know, remain hopelessly narrow, clogged and obstructed. The isolation and aloofness of the center of power away from the feedback of the multiple voices is not of recent making and is certainly not the work of present-day villains. "The arrogance of power" and its reciprocal, the "paralysis of the many" in whose behalf it is presumably exercised, is probably a built-in feature of any form of government, democracy included. In America, this "predicament" may have been blunted and obscured by a 150-year-old tradition that has conditioned us to "consent not to consent" all the time. The "outs" have learned to wait until they are "in" and the "ins" are always prepared to be thrown out. This politics of the "revolving door" served America well for it taught us to accept compromise as a way of life. The same tradition has also camouflaged some of the limitations of our political institutions. It has made us overestimate the capacities of our formulas of democracy to safeguard our liberties while at the same time retaining sufficient power to govern.

Historians may continue to argue whether the isolation of those in power from their constituents is really a new trend of modern history, or whether recent history has merely expanded the awareness of it. The realization that has slowly emerged during the last ten years that democracy Western-style is *not* always synonymous with the "rule of the people" came as a profound shock to many of us. The experts in political theory and philosophy of government have told us of course all along that democracy never implied rule of all the people and that, in fact, in any country that is too large or complex to be governed by town hall meetings, the translation into practice of such a concept would lead to the absurd.

> "Perhaps the most important reason for the malaise is that the new expectations are developing in an old economic and political system which cannot really deal with them. We are, after all, still a very unequal society, in which income and power are highly centralized. Though everyone's income has risen in the last 20 years, five per cent of the people still earn about 22 per cent of the annual income; one per cent own more than a third of the nation's total assets, and the 200 largest corporations do a majority of the nation's business. Government is equally centralized; it is more responsive to its own bureaucracies and to the most well-funded and highly organized interest groups than to other citizens; more to businessmen than consumers; and more to suppliers of military hardware than to advocates of peaceful soft ware.

> "This state of affairs is less a result of conspiracy than of past arrangements; it reflects an older society in which popular expectations were lower and few people expected either the economy or the Government to

meet their wishes and needs. Consequently, they remained politically inactive, and both the corporations and the Government responded mainly to groups which already had high expectations, developing centralized decision-making routines which they are now not always able or willing to change.

"Ralph Nader and others are fighting hard to make the corporate and governmental apparatuses more accountable to the general public, and their success so far could not have been achieved without the favorable climate in which they are working. At the same time, greater success is held back in part by some traditional attitudes that support the existing centralization. For one thing, many people do not care how public decisions are made as long as these decisions benefit them. Others still believe sufficiently in laissez-faire to oppose public intervention in the operations of business, although this belief is much less intense than it was only a few years ago. And many more doubt that even a more accountable Government could improve their standard of living, for they continue to see it as their enemy, which demands taxes for wasteful expenditures which do not benefit them and which they would rather spend privately.

"Still, there is enough public dissatisfaction about centralization to create a feeling among people that they are powerless and increasingly so, that they cannot bring about change even if they wanted to — and this too contributes to malaise. To some extent, their judgment is accurate; as bureaucracies become more important and corporations larger, the centers of power are harder to reach and, of course, as more people want a voice, each voice must, by simple arithmetic, become less powerful. Nevertheless, some of the feelings of powerlessness are themselves a consequence of higher expectations. When people did not demand power, they did not realize how powerless they were, and only now that they want it do they feel that they are powerless — and unhappy."[9]

Being ignored is certainly a relatively new experience for the literate, educated and articulate members of our society who had been accustomed to volunteer advice on anything and everything which, although it was not always followed, was at least listened to. The frustration they experience now is probably no different than the frustration that must have been part of the life of the "conservatives" in the day of Roosevelt; only they directed their fury against "that man in the White House" but were too "loyal" to question the institution just because those who were in charge could govern without benfit of their advice.

After years of marches, protest demonstrations, anti-war moratoria, boycotts, teach-ins, vigils, rallys, and bivouacs, both those who have participated in them as well as those who have watched them from a distance are left with the uncomfortable suspicion that these were perhaps exercises in letting off steam and as such, quite satisfactory, but that these activities had made no impact at all on the course of history. The picture of our recent president once proudly proclaiming that he would turn on a football game on television to drown out the voices of anti-war youth who were pleading with him to please not send them to their death in Vietnam haunts us. Perhaps other members of the power elite who were entrusted with the privilege of ruling and decision-making, keep the curtains drawn and their rooms soundproofed so that they too can carry on the business of governing without distraction from outside noises. But perhaps these fears are

_____

9. Herbert J. Gans, "The American Malaise," New York Times Magazine, February 6, 1972.

unfounded. When the history of our turbulent decade will be written, it may well be established that the shouting and the screaming and the marching was effective after all in a sort of intangible way, just as a continuous dripping of water can cause a rock to split.

Protest demonstrations, boycotts, strikes, sit-ins, marches and moratoria are really not as new nor as recent as they seem. They have been for a long time part of the strategy of minority groups who have no other access to government. More influential groups can and always have communicated their demands more effectively though less noisily. The fact that these strategies have been pursued in the past by minorities so tiny that they have barely made an impact and have now been adopted by an ever-widening circle of dissatisfied members of our society, adds proof that the feeling of voicelessness is spreading and in direct proportion to its spread more desperate means are being sought to amplify a message that otherwise won't seem to get through.

It may well turn out that the protest marches and boycotts, the teach-ins and the vigils are to be the archetypal, first immature but long overdue attempts to replace the missing component that was lost when, under the pressure of population growth and distribution in modern industrial societies, democracy was transformed from popular government to representative government.

Obviously, equal participation even in local decision-making is impossible in modern states composed largely of huge urban communities. It is not even the most important goal to be desired in "democratic" societies such as the United States where less than 50% are actually participating in the single opportunity offered them to influence policies, namely, the exercise of their vote. But voting is only the "court of last resort," an act which, to many, may not mean as much as the opportunity to participate in the search for solutions or to exercise their imagination for the advancement of the common welfare. Since the disappearance of the town hall meetings, there is really no forum available to so-called "ordinary people," and the collective imagination or "wisdom of the people" to which every politician pays deferential lip service, has been effectively immobilized. This, in spite of television debates, radio talkathons, and letters to the editors of prestigious and not-so-prestigious newspapers which resemble a tiresome merry-go-round on which the same famous and often infamous people reappear at periodic intervals to sound off, no matter how mistaken their judgment may have been in the past. The rest of us are polled from time to time by opinion researchers who try to elicit from us "yes" or "no" answers to preincubated questions, an exercise that hardly calls forth our best mental faculties.

To people who feel that they are wronged, threatened, restrained, misused and not represented by their government, the only thing worse than the anger that provokes them to shout is the realization that their shouts are not being heard. One may honestly argue that the signals the dissenters devised to make themselves heard, including the more desperate attempts such as nuisance demonstrations, flag burnings and boycots, were not only faulty but totally ineffective means of amplifying their message; but can anyone point out to them what other effective alternatives are available to them to make themselves heard? Are the legitimate channels sufficiently unplugged to give feedback to the decision makers of anything but the most garbled messages? The proposals advanced by the far our revolutionaries to cure that syndrome, were very simple and like most simple solutions quite unacceptable to the rest of us. They called for a radical shift of power away from those who hold it. Their slogan was "power to the people." But that is merely another way of extending franchise to one group by disenfranchising another. Reformers and revolutionaries in the past have unfortunately developed the annoying habit of invariably becoming more autocratic than the tyrannies they started out to replace. There was little in the program of the Far Left that promised they would be an exception to this rule, nor did their manners encourage any illusions about the nature of the total tyranny that SDS, Weathermen or Panthers would have imposed on us, if in the process of eliminating whatever ails us now, they had succeeded in "dumping the baby with the bath" and robbed us of our traditional liberties and constitutional safeguards.

Liberals have advanced their own less dramatic cure. Their panacea was to promote justice and equality by providing for a broadening of the base, by helping the weak to become strong or by increasing the number of pressure groups by moving the "outs" of society to a more "inside" position and then pushing them across the dividing line from that of disenfranchised to one of influence and representation. Once this is accomplished, liberals find it difficult to forgive their former clients who have learned their lessons too well and have proceeded to act like men of power themselves. Thus their wrath is turned now against the unions because union leaders have learned this lesson and are known to play like equal partners in the jungle game of economics, much as their opposites in the NAM. Some liberals are already beginning to resent the Blacks because they refuse to act like underdogs, and sponsor their own cause without benefit of white liberal advice.

> "All the (liberal) dissenter needs is someone who is suffering, a victim that he can help. Since the Six Day War, he has found it difficult to forgive the Jews for no longer being downtrodden. Victorious Jews do not make good subjects for crucifixion. The rapidity with which some of Israel's friends have dropped that country, without bothering to analyze in detail the causes of the 1967 conflict, indicates that being pro-Israel has lost its power to absolve from guilt. By the same token, we can easily see why it is necessary for workers to be miserable. 'Are you hungry?' students asked the striking workers at the Renault plant — to the astonish-

ment, and amusement, of the workers. If the workers are happy, they can no longer be the dissenter's means of redemption."[10]

I think Revel caught what the "Strum and Drang" for an expanding democracy in this country was really about. Perhaps it is the second time in American history that a Frenchman recognized the American mind better than the natives did themselves (de Toqueville being the first). Revel's words will have strong appeal to young Americans for he rationalized a kind of mystical belief shared by most Americans in the so-called "wisdom of the people." The search was on for a way to tap that treasure not only as a last resort to bail us out, but to provoke it continuously by stirring what Revel calls the "collective imagination" to make life more satisfactory and rewarding for the largest number of people.

"Freedom should not be viewed only as a relationship between the individual and his rulers. Seen under that aspect, freedom is an abstraction — and an abstraction that has become a target in the academicians' criticism of liberalism. The relationship between the governor and the governed is only the framework for something much larger, for a complex of elements which includes, above all, participation by the collective intelligence of the people in the governing (or the subversion) of a society. It may be that this was the secret of the 'break-through' by the countries involved in the first world revolution; for those countries allowed their government to be influenced, in one way or another, by the creative contributions of a large number of its citizens; and the governments then made use of those contributions in the management and mo-

---

10. From J. F. Revel's "Without Marx or Jesus," Doubleday and Company, 1971.

dification of public affairs. Therefore, to speak of freedom only in terms of 'guarantees' between people and government is like describing a great laboratory in terms of its unions and its pension plan. Certainly, unions and fringe benefits are important to the laboratory's researchers as an affirmation of their rights. But in today's societies, every citizen is assuming more and more the role of a researcher; that is, of a seeker after truth; and many people suffer as much because nobody is listening as they do because they are under-paid. Moreover, they feel that they are being underpaid because nobody is listening to them. A society to which nobody is listening is an oligarchy — and a society ruled by oligarchs will dry up and rot away because, statiscally, four or five men can have fewer new ideas than a hundred million men. When a citizen cannot criticize a worthless political or economic policy without being sent to prison, then the whole of that society is in danger — not only because one of its members has been subjected to 'an intolerable violation of the rights of the individual,' but also because a workable alternate policy may have been lost and buried forever. Revolution, obviously, must include socialization of the imagination."[11]

The memory of the town hall style of democracy, though never experienced by members of this generation, still fills us with a strong sense of nostalgia. But the town hall style of self-government is a paradise lost. It can never be resurrected again.

The media, both press and TV, certainly have missed their chance to take over the function when the "town hall" closed. They failed to advance the socialization of the "col-

_____

11. Jean-Francois Revel's "Without Marx or Jesus," Doubleday and Company, 1971.

lective imagination" and they certainly did nothing to provoke the "wisdom of the people." There were no counterparts to the Ted Mack or Ed Sullivan amateur discoveries on the political shows. Both TV and press merely offered themselves as forums to the same spokesman over and over again to either repeat or revise themselves as the years went by, or they flooded us with preincubated poll questions which challenged our prejudices but not our social imagination or resourcefulness.

New channels and mechanisms will have to be designed to translate into reality what Revel poetically calls "the socialization of the imagination." Possibly massive decentralization may advance this goal. It may well be the 540 Congressional delegates are not an adequate number to represent 200 million people, particularly when ideas are to be fed back and forth. Perhaps the function of a representative may change from that of taking on the burden of contemplating legislative solutions to political problems to one who actively solicits and stimulates the search for political truth from all who care to participate and thus provide a forum for those who wish to be heard and taken seriously.

What we want most of our political institutions is a means of protection against the arbitrariness and inequities of life and of nature, to which we still are exposed in spite of, or possibly because of, the complexities of our civilization. Life, as John F. Kennedy once pointed out, is inherently unfair. Our social institutions should serve to blunt the natural inequities to which we are prone, not to add to them. So we thought in the days of the New Deal. Some of our own ideals seem to have been resurrected again by our sons and daughters, though they would never admit it. But as it became increasingly impossible to advance our economic pursuits like independent "craftsmen," and as we were required to conform with a set of rules growing steadily in complexity, the jealousy with which we wish to maintain the independence of the "private reserve" grew with a passion and a vengeance.

It is interesting that the mood of resistance to the invasion of government into private lives is shared to some extent also by the younger members of the other side of the Iron Curtain. There is considerable tolerance to regimentation with the less private aspects of community existence. Thus Communist youth rarely object to socialistic management of their economic pursuits, but resent most bitterly the restrictions on their movements and interference with their thoughts through censorship and travel restrictions.

In America, the draft had become the great symbol of government tyranny. To the English, French and German student generation, the minister of education was the villain who, through a system of the so-called 11+ entrance examinations could funnel youth out of careers long before they have had a chance to find themselves.

In the meantime, the new generation follows Emerson's advice that the best government is one that governs least. By this criterion, most contemporary governments, including the Democratic ones, would flunk the test. One wonders how successful the experiment in individual freedom which Thoreau conducted in Walden Pond could be repeated in present-day America. Chances are that Walden Pond is polluted and the young hermit in search of his soul there would be harassed by so many ordinances, he would have had to take a lawyer along to keep abreast of them.

The essence of democracy is still intelligent cooperation and the tradition of democracy is anchored to that time-honored STOP sign erected at the border of the private preserve across which no government shall trespass. The classes of 1968-1973 were not disposed to advocate that the "off limits" line be moved backward.

The Roots in Science

I

To imply that the new humanism has roots in science seems a bit redundant in the face of the disillusionment with science that is increasingly voiced by those who call themselves humanists. Many of the young who are among the loudest proponents of the new mood, make no secret of their deep distrust of science. Since, by their own admission, they neither want to analyze nor to manage the world, but want to experience it, they find science at the very least irrelevant and at worst evil. Granted that science is no longer the sacred cow it used to be 20 years ago and that the reputation it once enjoyed is considerably tarnished, it is still being invoked to justify and reinforce practically every ideology which moved men's mind in the 20th century. The more thoughtful proponents of change feel that the salvation of the human race, particularly if he is to be rescued from his worst enemy — himself — will be accomplished only by the application of the scientific method, or certainly with a strong and powerful assist from it. All modern ideologies and blueprints for a new and better social order seek from science proof and confirmation that their basic premises about the nature of man or of society are correct, much in the manner in which previously new religious doctrines and heresies rested their case on an appeal that their unorthodox views were really based on a more correct interpretation of the word of God.

The two most ambitious modern programs designed for the improvement of the human condition, socialism and psychoanalysis, claim to be scientific disciplines per se and reserve for their propositions and axioms the status of scientific law. The old question that occupied the minds of proponents of earlier ideologies, namely, whether man's nature is compatible with the specific goals they set for him is lately being revived by those advocates of change who seek a more humane way of life and a more compassionate social order.

Implicit in all the arrangements that call for action to change man's relationship to man, is of course the presupposition that within limits man can be changed and modified, or to put it in more poetic terms, that "Man can be good, is inherently good, and that this goodness can be freed and realized."

Socialism, Psychoanalysis, Religion, all suggest levers of liberating màn to unselfish "Goodness" either by shifting material conditions in a classless society, or by creating a sane community of "adjusted" members, or by appeals for conformity with and participation in the master plan of an absolute authority. Interestingly enough, modern humanists stimulated perhaps by the remarkable success of the life sciences during the last two decades turn hopefully to biology rather than to psychology or economics for confirmation of what they optimistically believe is the "true nature of Man."

The old question about the nature of man has been reformulated into terms borrowed from the language of communication science of which modern biology is so fond. The question is being asked, "Is man genetically programmed for collaboration and cooperation or is he programmed for aggression, competition and war?" A growing number of biologists have addressed themselves to the question of whether the study of man's biological potential indicates that his capacity for collaboration, compassion and humanization can be expanded or whether in fact it has already reached its limits, so that under the strain of our present civilization, like an over-stretched rubber band, it is more likely to recoil backward than to expand. Reference is made to the books of Desmond Morris' "The Naked Ape" and "The Human Zoo,"

B. F. Skinner's "Beyond Freedom and Dignity," Konrad Lorenz' "On Aggression," Jacques Monod's "Chance and Necessity" and Alexander Allard's "The Human Imperative."

Interestingly enough the answers that are emerging from these studies need not disturb those who want to believe in the perfectability of man nor do they reinforce those who, in the name of a science which they do not fully understand, insist that civilization, culture, religion and morality are at best nice cosmetics which even if very generously applied, rub off easily. Civilization, the latter insist, is at best plastic surgery. It can not transform an animal into anything but another animal.

For many it is still fashionable to prove their intellectual virility by accepting as self-evident truth the conclusion that:

> "Man isn't a noble savage, he's an ignoble savage. He is irrational, brutal, weak, silly, unable to be objective about anything where his own interests are involved. . . . The brutal and violent nature of man . . . is a true picture of him; and any attempt to create social institutions on a false view of the nature of man is probably doomed to failure."[1]

Unfortunately, past attempts by biologists to provide a kind of rational and scientific justification for social, ethical and political goals have, as a rule, not stood up well to close and critical scrutiny. The crossing of the divide that separates strict scientific factual analysis of naturalistic processes from their philosophical and ethical implications imposes upon the scientist, indeed, an awful responsibility, not only because of the nonsense that can be written, but because of the consequences inherent if that nonsense ever becomes a call for ac-

---

1. Stanley Kubrick, quoted in an interview with the New York Times.

tion. The example of the Nazis teaches us, if anything, to be rather more than less wary about the "crossing of the divide" that separates scientific from humane methods of inquiry. The writings of men like Austin Chamberlain, Ezra Pound, Friedrich Nietzsche, Wyndham Lewis and for that matter the whole school of Eugenics has brought Auschwitz that much closer, but even if Auschwitz had never happened one would still have to admit that the excursion of theologians, philosophers, artists, social commentators, and political and moral ideologists into biological science in search of confirmation for their doctrines and vice versa has not aways been a blessing for either.

To paraphrase Medawar:

"People who have brandished naturalistic principles at us in the past, have usually been up to no good. Think of only what we have suffered from a belief in the existence and overriding authority of the fighting instinct, from the doctrines of racial superiority, the metaphysics of blood and soil, from the belief that warfare between men or nations represents fulfillment of historical as well as biological laws."

A good deal of that confusion was undoubtedly brought about by the introduction of phrases like "Struggle for Existence," "Natural Selection," "Competition," and "Survival of the Fittest," which had ethical, ideological and political repercussions created largely in the minds of those who did not understand Darwin and modern biology at all.

If the interpretation derived from classical Darwinism was indeed based on misunderstanding of anything reputable biologists had ever proclaimed about the operational forces

----

2. Peter Medawar, "The Future of Man." Basic Books, N.Y., 1959.

90

guiding evolution, then it may be profitable to try once more to fit the models and concepts derived from the life sciences and from the theory of evolution to the study of history.

II

In bare outline, the mechanism of evolution as seen by the geneticist runs as follows: Mutations, or changes in the gene material arise in every animal species with a certain finite frequency and thus supply the raw material for evolution. Most mutations, being accidents of nature, are more likely to be deleterious than beneficial at the time they occur. They may cause a change in the structure of one of the organs, or they may simply change the rate of a physiological process, rendering the affected organism more susceptible to disease or metabolic failure. Some mutations may affect the coloration of all or some external parts of the body (skin, eye color, hair color), others may affect the size, shape or structure of bodyparts (cleft palate, hydrocephalus), while still others may just affect purely physiological reactions like irritability, rate of metabolism or glandular secretion (hemophilia, Parkinsonism, pituitary dwarfism). But while most mutations, because of their deleterious effects, would be expected to be lost by simply impairing the afflicted animals in their competition with healthier members of their species, they have a way of being maintained and perpetuated in the population. This is probably due to the circumstance that newly mutated genes are usually not permitted to express themselves in the presence of the homologous older normal gene on the other chromosome of the pair. This relationship is referred to among geneticists as "recessivity," a term denoting the fact that genes are present in each cell in pairs, and if one of the pair changes (i.e. mutates) the other unchanged members of the pair as a rule still exert the dominant influence. The majority of the so-called "visible mutants" resulting from the random union of two mutated genes, can at best give us an inkling of the far higher frequency of the number of such mutated genes present, though hidden, in the population by virtue of their recessivity.

Ultimately however the success or failure of a gene to maintain itself in a population depends upon the "selective" action of the environment to which all biological variations are exposed. The more "fit" genes survive in greater numbers than the less "fit." It is important to realize however that fitness is defined in terms of the environment. There is no such thing as fitness per se. In the regions of Africa where it lives, the giraffe with long legs and a long neck is more fit than a stubbier giraffe. If the giraffe were transported to the arctic tundra, where all food grows within a few inches of the ground, its great height would no longer make it more fit, but rather less so. Fitness then of a gene or its mutated allele is a property conveyed upon it by the environment. It is a value as changeable as the environment itself.

The essentials of the relationship between environment and biological variants was first proposed in scientifically acceptable form by Charles Darwin in 1859 in his "Origin of Species by Natural Selection." His theory of selection can be reduced to the simple logical proposition "that those variants which are better adapted to their environment will reproduce in greater numbers" than their less favored contemporaries. Darwin's theory of natural selection is really no theory at all. It is merely a statement of the observation that some organisms survive and others do not. The theory gives us no information as to how some organisms persist and other fail to do so.

It fell to the science of genetics to provide the explanation of the mechanism through which evolution operates. This new theory which supplements Darwin's is called by T. Huxley: "Evolution, the modern synthesis" and it was formulated mainly by the insights and in the language of modern genetics.

Evolution, then may be conceived of as a resultant between two fundamental biological phenomena.

a) The raw material of evolution is provided by a discrete number of accidents (mutations) which presumably occur during gene reduplication. Each results in ever so slight changes in the germ plasm, which in their totality give rise to the whole store of biological variations.

b) The direction of evolution is determined by the environmental situation within which the organism has to accommodate itself. In biology we have come to personalize this "tete a tete" between a biological population and its environment by referring to it as "Natural Selection." Natural Selection however is not an all or none proposition. Unlike "artificial selection" as practiced by a breeder, natural selection is merely a difference of survival of competing genotypes and often this difference is exceedingly slight.

But the "bad" genes of today may become the most desirable genes in the changed environment of tomorrow. It would be nice if organisms were able to respond to the changes of its environment by producing only the proper genetic alterations when needed. Nature however has hit upon a different solution. Instead of discarding the accidents which happen during the difficult process of gene duplication (i.e. mutations), it preserves them, shielded by the protective cover of recessivity, for future use. The greater the genetic variability produced in this manner within species, the greater the choice of switches into which a species can be directed in response to changing environments.

The risks are obvious. By allowing possibly deleterious mutations to "hide behind" the dominant "normal" allele, and thus protecting them from total extinction, a species population may accumulate an ever-growing number of deleterious genes.

It is a gamble, but a gamble which apparently must be taken.

A few examples taken from observations of microbiology, paleontology and anthropology may illustrate the point.

If a population of bacteria like Escherichia coli (the ordinary symbiont type inhabiting the colon of men) is cultured in the presence of the mold Pencillium or Streptomycin, multiplication of the cells in the culture will soon cease, and all the members of the bacterial population will die. Occasionally a bacterial cell survives despite the presence of such actinomycetes. From such a survivor a new strain of bacteria may develop which may be completely resistant to the bactericidal substance produced by the mold. These observations may be interpreted in one of two ways. One might account for the change by assuming that the presence of Penicillium itself induced the mutation confering resistance or at least accelerating its rate of occurrence.

The alternate hypothesis explains the change by assuming that mutations conveying resistance to Penicillium have occurred in bacteria from time to time regardless of whether the strain was exposed to the mold or not. In the absence of the mold the resistant mutants have held no advantage over the ancestral susceptible form. They may even have a slight disadvantage, because the same gene responsible for resistance may have other yet unknown side effects.

When exposed to penicillin the obvious happens: All the susceptible cells succumb, leaving only the few of the randomly arisen resistant mutants to survive and reproduce, thus transforming the original susceptible strain into a resistant one.

The genetic reinterpretation of Darwinism has thus given an explanation of evolution so that it can now actually be "repeated in the test tube," as the example from microbiology illustrates. The new genetic synthesis of evolution has provided also the key by which the transformations of species and their descent from one another as recorded in the paleontological past, can rationally be fitted together.

Although the paleontological record presents us with remains in which only abrupt and discontinuous changes are observable, most students of the fossil record agree that these changes must have been preceded by a slow and gradual accumulation of merphological variants, which though invisible to the paleontologist, were nevertheless real.

The construction of the fleshy lobed fin, which enabled certain crossopterygian fishes to seek terrestrial surroundings during the Devonian period must have been preceded by an accumulation of a fantastic number of mutated genes at a time when any deviation from a primarily fin ray type could only have been disadvantageous.

The simultaneous accumulation in those fishes of a large block of mutated genes, which in their additive effect resulted in a saclike outpocketing from the gut, the lung, which could serve for exchange of gases from the air, rather than of gases dissolved in water, as is the customary situation in gills, gave the crossopterygian fishes their unique advantage during the severe droughts of the Devonian period.

A final example from anthropology. Like other plant or animal species Homo sapiens have diverged genetically in several environments in which different human groups have come to settle. However, unlike other animal species, the isolation between these groups was never complete enough to prohibit interbreeding and therefore free gene flow. As a result the accumulation of gentic differences was never of a sufficient magnitude to allow species separation in "Homo sapiens." But the different environments selected different genes giving rise to at least five distinct racial types, distinguished by the frequency with which certain genes are present in their population.

We do not know why it might be better to have frizzy hair if one lives in Africa. But we know at least something about the value of one of the most obvious and dramatic racial characteristics in man, the presence and quantitative distribution of pigment cells. It is evident that in an environment where sunshine is intense and prolonged the presence of cells in the skin endowed with an enzyme system capable of synthesizing pigment granules in response to exposure to the rays of the ultraviolet spectrum is of considerable advantage. It is reasonable to assume then that in the native population of Africa the frequency of all those genes directing the differentiation of a large number of pigment cells would be far greater than in the nordic population of Scandinavia.

In Africa, therefore, a block of genes assuring heavy pigment production in the skin at all times has been selected for, while in more temperate climates characterized by seasonal variation, a more plastic pigment setup is established where the pigment forming reaction is started upon exposure to the sun's spectrum and lost in its absence.

The fundamental difference between this and the Lamarckian scheme (according to which organisms invent new structures and modes of functioning in direct, adaptive responses to change) often escapes those unfamiliar with contemporary genetics. The genetic interpretation has indeed made short shrift of the teleological argument popularized by Lamarck. Life, or living organisms, do not deliberately and purposefully respond to external stimuli by modifying their equipment into structures more capable of meeting new situations, in the way that a corporation may attempt to meet the pressure of rising competition by reshuffling its table or organization. Actually, if some changes occur in nature in this way they can be shown to be only transitory. Thus, to quote one classic experiment, Weissmann cut off a great many mouse tails without ever succeeding to produce a race of tail-less mice.

There isn't a species alive today, which could not have been improved upon, if we choose to play God. If we look long enough, we probably find in every group of plants or animals some kind of "error of judgment" or some construction-blunder or inconsistency.

Medawar, in his "Future of Man," cities the example of the evolution of immunological defenses long before the coming of mammals. "Mammals are viviparous, the young are nourished for some time within the body of the mother, a truly remarkable and clever innovation, but the device unfortunately also raised the unpleasant prospect that the mother might react immunologically upon her unborn children and might treat them as foreign bodies. This mistake has cost the life of one in 150 children before the arrival of modern medicine."

"Mother Nature" obviously does not always know best. Evolution, itself, is a story of waste, makeshift, compromise, and blunder. "She" sometimes acts wisely, but often foolishly at least by human standards of perfection or efficiency. With just a few tricks in her bag and a limited repertoire at her disposal "she" brings about the considerable variety of life, which we all so admire, but "she" does this much in the manner of an old lady, who constantly rearranges her antiquated furniture, but rarely adds anything new. Bones that were meant to hold up the jaw in elasmobranch fishes are transposed into the middle ear of mammals to serve as amplifiers for sound. Air bladders originally meant to keep fishes afloat are rerouted to serve as lungs for exchange of gases of terrestrial animals.

If one insists on looking for "purpose in life," one might as well be satisfied with the realization that "life" appears to anticipate a whole set of possible conditions which may or may not arise and that "it" gets ready for them by making the necessary provisions by way of genetic "freaks" which, if not of much use at one time, may touch off the most useful genetic re-groupings at dramatic periods of large-scale environmental change. To put the matter paradoxically, freaks have a future and the blessings of the fully "adjusted" organism cannot last longer than the context within which they are studied.

The take home lesson of all these considerations is this — There is no *single* technique of biological survival. The predatory acts that are so highly developed in some vertebrates serve some species, skill in camouflage may serve others, and collaboration may serve still others. The way of the tiger as well as the way of the spider, or the fox or the ant, are equally promising strategies for survival.

Assuming that survival value may be the only measuring rod, against which all codes and value judgments of conduct must ultimately be tested (and that in itself may be a point of controversy), biology teaches us that there are many different patterns by which species manage to survive. Some types of living arrangement will make for survival in one group, but lead to extinction in another. Traits, useful for conflict and competitive strategy, have as much survival value as traits promoting cooperation. Appeals for reinforcement of either trait in behaviour can, of course, be made, but never be justified per se by biology.

The only strategy of survival for "Homo sapiens" is neither imitation of the ways that serve the tiger, nor those that serve insects. The future of man is inextricably linked to culture.

If the biologist wishes to advocate or justify schemes of conduct or programs of social action and reject others in the light of his special knowledge, he must do better than just point to the living arrangement of some successful species and suggest.

There is, however, one common trick to survival and all species that beat extinction had to learn it. Too rigid a specialization at the expense of variability will spell doom and certain extinction. Only a population that builds within its genetic pool enough genetic variability to be ready with new adaptation if and when the environment changes can hope to persist.

All of this may seem totally irrelevant for man. Man has obviously moved far beyond the limits and boundaries of the ecological niche into which he was initially placed when he first evolved from some common ancestor, whom he shared with his cousins the apes. Civilization has taken him out of the game of evolution at least up to a point. There is, however, some merit to compare biological and cultural survival patterns if for no other reason than to see whether the two are comparable at all.

It may be both fun and informative to see whether biology in its most advanced version can offer conceptual models for interpreting historical processes and in doing so offer a strategy for survival of civilized man.

III

Spengler, it may be recalled, had proposed that civilizations or cultures be conceived as organisms undergoing youth, maturity and unavoidable decline and death. Suggestive as many of the conclusions which Spengler had drawn from his thesis may be, a growing number of historians have found it ever more difficult to overlook the rather far reaching difference between organism and society upon which Spengler's thesis is erected. Instead we shall turn to a more recent "Study of History," namely Toynbee's conception of a "society-civilization."

Toynbee's conception of history resembles Spengler's with civilization going through the same cycles. He differs from Spengler in denying that this process is predetermined.

But the essential outlines of the process, namely the birth of a civilization, its growth and differentiation and its subsequent failure to adjust to a new challenge, leading to its subsequent breakdown, have been repeated according to Toynbee 21 times throughout recorded history. Only five of these civilizations are listed as surviving, in the sense that they have not yet reached the stage of inner breakdown, though a number of them seem to be approaching their own destruction rather rapidly. These survivors include: the Western, the Hindu, the Islamic, the Far Eastern and the Orthodox Byzantine civilizations. The list of the less fortunate victims includes: the Egyptian, the Andean, the Sinic, the Minoan, the Sumeric, the Mayan, the Yucatec, the Mexic, the Hittite, the Syriac, the Babylonic and the Hellenic.

The genesis of each of these civilizations is conceived by

Toynbee as the outcome of a unique, rather heroic group response of a community to the challenge of fairly difficult, unpleasant and unusual situations. Often the adverse stimulus is provided by the terrain, such as the barrenness of the land which started Minoan and Hellenic cultures.

A more recent example of terrain directing the birth of a nation may be the experience and efforts of a group of Puritan refugees who settled along the coast of New England 300 years ago.

Other effective challenges which organize a herd of people into a community able to master its surroundings and assure its collective survival are: pressures from outside enemies, such as was experienced by the Iberian Christians from their neighbors the Moors; penalization such as was applied to the Jews of the Diaspora. Even slavery has provided adequate challenges with creative consequences.

Once established, a new community will have to add something to its bag of tricks in addition to whatever new inventions were responsible for it emerging successfully in the first place. The conquest over its adversaries, whether in the form of an outside oppressor, enemy or just rough terrain, must be followed by less dramatic accomplishments of building a state, a society or a way of group living. A community must make arrangements to assure its continued existence by organizing itself, making laws, writing constitutions, setting up governments and establishing rules of conduct and norms of action. This phase of the life cycle of a civilization is designated by Toynbee as its "Growth and Differentiation."

Growth and differentiation are dependent on the emergence of what Toynbee calls the "creative minorities," who must come up with the ideas by which to shape governments, strategies, social contracts, codes of laws and ethics.

The emergence of a multiplicity of voices in the form of creative minorities should endow the community with a polymorphism of its own which would guarantee that new solutions can be found to meet new challenges if and when they present themselves.

Unfortunately, on that score the record of history Toynbee recites is not too reassuring. The leaders who successfully responded to one challenge are rarely the successful respondents to the next. Those who have succeeded once are apt on the next occasion to be found resting on their oars.

While this brief paragraph certainly does not adequately state Toynbee's thesis, it may suffice to convey the similarity of his conception of a "society-civilization" with the biological "species population."

However, the biological parallel is to Lamarck, not Darwin, and not to the evolutionary synthesis as formulated by the science of genetics.

IV

In what follows, I should like to sugest in the roughest outline how the historians might bring their biological model-thinking up to date. The first thing that would become apparent is that questions of absolute origin, or of first "causes" of ancestral civilization would continue to elude our methods. As of now, biology cannot satisfactorily answer the question of how life ever got started, but it can both describe and explain how subsequent life-forms connect up with previous ones. Analogously, we may be able to explain how successor-civilizations succeeded where their predecessors failed. What we cannot explain is why man, at one particular time, should have become a culture-building animal. Not that there is any scarcity of speculation on such matters which have intrigued and continue to intrigue man's imagination though his available knowledge is not yet equipped to satisfy his curiosity on this point respectably.

In biology we have learned to live with this limitation ever since Pasteur's experiment proved rather conclusively that there is no such thing as "spontaneous generation" and that all living things come from previous living things.

With the issue of the "first" origin of cultural organizations shelved, how can we account for their survival or adaptation to an ever-changing environment? If culture-change is not clarified in the direct teleological Lamarckian fashion, perhaps on the social level there takes place some sort of "cultural selection" of social mutants? Just as a biological species, prepares itself against a variety of unpleasant and possibly lethal external changes by permitting in its population a pool of randomly mutated genes (fit to meet such emergencies), so perhaps each society must harbor in its midst its own contingent of "mutants" or "irregulars," called respectively freaks, misfits, deviants, radicals or non-conformists.

Now, the existence of such non-conforming minorities within the framework of any existing (and past) society is surely not a new discovery. Their role in all sorts of historical processes has intrigued the biographically-inclined historian as much as it has aroused those of the "historical materialist" school of thought. The former contend that all of history is but the product of the non-conformist hero or "great personality" who imposed his or her visions upon the human multitude. According to the historical determinists, on the other hand, the "great men" function merely as the mouthpiece of social forces, at best riding the crest of a wave which they delude themselves into thinking they have personally created. The historical materialists are quite content to surmise that if Isaac Newton had never lived to see that legendary apple fall off the tree, some other British gentleman would have sooner or later observed some other fruit's descent from some other tree or arrived at similar conclusions by some analogous observations.

To evaluate properly the nature of the relationship between the individual and the non-conforming minorities on the one hand, and the social forces which interact with them in producing changed patterns of group living, on the other, we must not be misled by focusing too sharply upon such minorities as proved to be of major historical significance.

"Many are called but few are chosen." The ones who are "chosen," however, as carriers of new life-patterns, be they organic or social, turn out to be those who appear as "deviants" in the old patterns of (natural or social) environments. In biological terminology, the non-adjusted individuals might be called "social mutants."

Having established the existence of a fair sized potential stock of "social mutants" we must turn our attention to two questions: 1) What manner of circumstances is involved in creating such social mutants and 2) What forces determine their eventual success of failure in shaping historical events to their liking? The answer to both of these questions is, "We do not know." The question as to why some members of a social order are always prevented from finding their peculiar needs gratified within the arrangements permissible at given times and places is as fascinating and unanswerable as the question about the nature of the processes leading to gene mutations. All we know of the latter is that they happen continuously and spontaneously and that under certain conditions, such as radiation, e.g., they will occur with sharply increased frequency. In other words, mutations are accidents and accidents happen. Analogously, we have not yet hit upon a satisfactory theory which would explain the chain of events by which an individual is alienated from his group within which he was nourished. In the absence of confirmable theory, there is, of course, speculation. Thus we are told that a sudden and miraculous enlightenment on the road to Damascus changed Paul of Tarsus from a leading member of the Jewish upper-class to a converted and converting hermit in the Arabian desert. The sacking of Kapilavastu presumably so impressed the young aristocrat Siddharta Gautama that he renounced a world which appeared to become inhospitable to aristocrats and he thus was motivated to attempt wihdrawal as a new and better form of life. Eloquent and powerful as are the figures of Paulus and Buddha, of Moses, Jesus, Mohammed, St. Augustine, Luther, Cromwell, Herzl, Lenin, Marx and Gandhi, of ultimately even greater significance is perhaps the less eloquent band of apostles, disciples, fighters and martyrs which make up the nucleus of the "great man's" effectiveness. If the great and lonely figures which lead into the future are the "macromutations," then the small minority, forming their initial followers, could be called the micro-mutable material. They form that strange collection of misfits, cranks, visionaries, impractical idealists and dreamers to whom perhaps Christ addressed himself when he said: "Thou art the salt of the earth and the leaven that makes the dough."

As regards the second question, we must profess an equal measure of ignorance.

The analogy to biology here is to the formula established for selection. Just as there are selective forces operating in biological speciation, "quasi-selective forces" might be at work in history.

In more articulate language, "selection" in a historical sense implies that under a different set of conditions, i.e., under a slightly different constellation of outside factors to which culture patterns are required to respond, the influence of a great personality or the outcome of a given historical adventure or movement might either have failed, or succeeded or taken on an entirely different direction from the one it actually did take.

We are told that the Roman Empire, during the long period of its decline, was fertile of large crops of prophets, Messiahs and other imports from the East, and the "Christians" were only one and, for some time, not even the most notable among others. One wonders whether the conversion of the Near Eastern population to Christianity which was just one of the many messianic sects flourishing at that time would have been as successful if the road system of the Roman Empire had been laid out less well. Fifteen hundred years later bids for religious change (and "salvation") were again advanced by such individuals and minority groups as the Waldigensers, Hussites, and Calvin, all of whom were of either small or of no major historical significance, but the Saxon monk Luther succeeded where the others had failed and it was he who brought on the "Reformation."

From among all sorts of proposed alternatives to "private enterprise" it was the bolshevists who carried the day and initiated a revolution, the end of which is not yet in sight. But communism as a way of living and organizing society and distributing goods has been proposed since time immemorial. Recall the Jewish Caldaeans, the followers of Christ, the Franciscan monks, the Utopian cooperatives in North America. None of these succeeded in setting up for any length of time a stable community in which property was owned collectively. Why were the bolshevists able to succeed where so many of their illustrious predecessors met only failure and frustration? Is the rise of constitutional government sufficiently explained by reference to English "genius" or "character," composed presumably of the hereditary material of Danish, Saxon and Norman "genius," none of which, however, in its own environment could foreshadow the kind of contractual relationship between crown and subjects eventually established by the Magna Carta in Runnymede in 1215. Perhaps similar aspirations entertained by some potential "rebels" of other nations did not find the same set of circumstances on the feudally organized continent to make such contract between King and nobles appealing and their ambitions ended, instead of in Parliament, at the Bastille.

V

To many historians the ultimate decline of practically all known civilizations points up better than any other factor the resemblance to organic life. No matter how triumphant a people's history and civilization, the ultimate fate of extinction and defeat is shared by all. So, at least, says Toynbee.

The similarity to biological laws is obvious – does not the story of paleontology reflect the coming and going of one species after another, much like history records the rise and fall of different civilizations?

But is extinction really in the cards for each and every civilization? Is Western civilization, in particular, approaching its "decline" or final agony, or its passage into a technologically monolithic power-structure as foreshadowed by new departures from Western norms in both the USSR and China? This question, if not answered, is raised again and again by serious-minded historians, taking their cue either from Spengler's earlier and gloomy prognosis for the "occident" or from Toynbee's detached recounting of all history as a series of unsuccessful civilization attempts to respond adequately to the ever-changing challenges of natural and social circumstances. Civilization's ball game with destiny scores a measly 21 to 5, according to Toynbee. Statistically this is indeed somewhat less than a good omen for the present.

Fortunately the biologists can provide a more balanced outlook. Few biologists will quarrel with the belief that all living organisms have limited life-spans, but no biologist is in possession of evidence which can be used for a proof that what holds for the individual organism must hold for the species. Many species, to be sure, have come and gone, but others have been around for a long time and their careers, if limited in the cosmological end, may have futures of as many millions of years as their past. By contrast, the human species, whether ultimately limited or not, has hardly started, instead of declining towards its "inevitable death." Thus, while death is a fact of life, there is nothing in evolutionary theory to indicate that extinction is the final end to which all evolution is mysteriously directed by some unfathomable power. Quite to the contrary, there appears on the time scale of biological evolution a large number of "Methuselahs" who seem to be strangely immune to extinction. Among the invertebrates particularly we have in the sea-shell "Lingula" an organism which is still amazingly like what it was 400 million years ago. The silica-secreting radiolaria are claimed to have existed since the Cambrian. An oyster of 200,000,000 years or more in the past would look quite familiar if served in a restaurant today. Among the vertebrate immortals, the reptilian Sphenodon deserves a place of honor, just as the oppossum which has survived unchanged since the Cretacious. The way to achieve or approach immortality, it seems, is to be fortunate in having made an early adaption to an environment which does not ever change, or to be ready with new adaptations where environmental changes cease to favor earlier conditions.

The one fatal fallacy which some of the otherwise most successful species have committed was to make too perfect an adaptation. By sacrificing versatility for perfection they failed to adapt to new environments. To make too complete an adjustment — putting all one's eggs in one basket — appears to be as lethal a course to take, as to make no adjustment at all.

The sabertoothed tiger, appearing in the early Oligocene became extinct only yesterday, i.e., in the Pleistocene, some 20 to 30 million years ago. According to Simpson, the ever-lengthening saber-tooth of this beast started out as a perfectly effective biting mechanism until eventually it became an impeding and destructive occlusion. The antlers of the Irish elks, which originally were highly adaptive weapons for offense and defense in the time became so cumbersome a burden that their owners were ultimately doomed before they had a chance to use them. "Study of History" is a storehouse of historical parallels to sabertoothed tigers and Irish elks.

The analogous fate of the knights in shining armour comes to mind. In the late Middle Ages they had perfected such all-protective "panzers" for themselves that, while shielded against blows and thrusts, they were also effectively imprisoned and immobilized and thus easy victims for more movable yeomen, fighting according to changing rules of combat.

The fate of the once-mighty Armada at the hands of the British pirate vessels is another case in point.

As the gist of all this, two lessons are respectfully offered: *1)* The final agony of all dying civilizations is marked by the desperate attempt to meet a crisis by too rigid a code. For society, just as for biological species, the inability to change beyond already successful changes, is the most general cause to which all more specific causes of downfall can be reduced. Rigidity, conformity, inflexibility spell extinction for societies as well as for organisms. The liberal mind may take some comfort from the historical lesson that demands of absolute obedience and conformity repeatedly made by society upon its members in time of trouble and crisis have rarely, if ever, succeeded in overcoming the difficulties for the sake of which they were invoked. Imperial absolutism, the Inquisition, the police-state or fascist dictatorship, they all have a way of succumbing in the end. *2)* Only the readiness to change offers promise of survival. Democracy as a form of government most likely to maximize change through multiple representation, may be defined as being itself one of the most potent, if not indispensable, social tools for providing optimal conditions for permitting and maximizing human diversity, filling the reservoir of social mutants whose presence and frequency co-varies with the success or failure of social organisms to meet unanticipated environmental changes from within or without. It is probably safe to say that given the correct momentum and frequency of change which instead of happening to man can now be produced by him in both deliberate and unforeseeable ways, there will be no society that can hope to survive without holding in readiness some of the "openness-to-change" which Western people attribute to democracy alone. The humanist-scientist will derive a certain amount of aesthetic elation from the idea that "democracy" is in phase with evolution, similar to the satisfaction that the philosophers of enlightenment must have experienced when they discovered that their natural and political philosophy derived from Natural Laws.

The truth that emerges from the loan of modern genetic conceptual models to social and moral theories is precisely the opposite of those pseudoscientific popular ideas nascent in the late nineteenth and twentieth century which proclaimed that social evolution is directed by what was presumed to be the biological law of survival of the fittest, that societies are organisms, which grow and must inevitably die, that competition between men, groups and nations is a necessary texture of all social organizations, because the same basic instincts that drive animals into social setups, also determine the "jungle type" relationship existing between its peers.

> "A parallel has often been pointed out between the evolution of a culture and the evolution of a species. Up to a point the parallel is useful. The culture represents a species. It is defined as an assemblage of practices representing the traits of a species. New practices arise for many reasons (they may be invented or they may come about by accident), and these are mutations to be tested by their contribution to the strength of the culture. The parallel breaks down at the critical point of transmission of practices. Cultural evolution is not only Lamarckian; an acquired characteristic may be taken by other 'species' as well. The concept of cultural evolution is important because it leads us to evaluate the strength of our own culture. Is a given form of government actually maintaining peace and security, domestically and internationally, in an effective way? Does it give its citizens freedom from attack by others? Is an economic system producing what the culture needs? Is education making the most of the genetic material born into the

culture? Are psychotherapeutic practices and institutions maintaining some kind of stability? And so on.

When we look at our culture in that way, we may be inclined to act. We may see changes which will lead to reinforcing consequences. The redesign of a culture is commonplace. Men invent new ways of teaching, new ways of raising children, new ways of collecting taxes, new ways of producing goods and so on. Most of these changes can be traced to personal goods or the goods of others, which we have already examined. But some of them may arise from a concern for the survival of the culture. But why should men be concerned about the survival of their culture? What difference does it make to young people in the last third of the twentieth century what the people who live in the last third of the twenty-first century will look like, what forms of government they will follow, what their literary or artistic interests may be? Certainly, no current goods in the sense of reinforcers can be derived from remote events of that kind. We are talking now not about what is good for the individual but about what is good for the culture. But how can the good of the culture be made good to the individual?

When young people ask, "Why should I care whether my culture survives?" the only honest answer seems to be this: There is no good reason, but if your culture has not convinced you there is, so much the worse for the culture. Somewhere in the process of the evolution of a culture, possibly for quite accidental reasons, the culture has begun to encourage its members to work for its survival. The sources of practices, as mutations, like the sources of biological mutations, are irrelevant. The important fact is the contribution to the strength of the culture. Those cultures which induce their members to work for their survival are, other things being equal, more likely to survive.

To change a culture, to increase its survival, one must answer three questions: (1) What are the conditions the culture must meet in order to survive? No one has formulated the answer in very clear terms. Even the emergencies to be met by a culture in the fairly near future are hard to predict. Tentative answers at least are, however necessary. (2) What kinds of behavior on the part of the members of the culture will be most effective in meeting these conditions? (3) What kind of social environment will produce such behavior?

We have made some progress in answering the last two questions. It is not impossible to identify kinds of behavior relevant to the solution of problems likely to be met by a culture and to design an environment likely to generate that behavior.

We are most likely to view the survival of a culture in competition with other cultures. We can visualize future emergencies in the form of the domination of world markets, military conquests, or the spread of a religion or economic system. When the Russians sent the first artificial satellite around the earth, it was not difficult to visualize a war in which a new technology might decide the issue. That was America's answer to question 1. What was needed in America was a comparable technology, and that was the answer to question 2. Better scientific education and training was the answer to question 3, and fairly substantial changes were made in support of scientific teaching. The unfortunate thing is that jingoistic nationalism, revealed religious truths, a commitment to historical determinism, or social Darwinism lead to narrow definitions of survival value and, therefore, a necessarily limited social design. They recognize only one of the contingencies of survival to be faced by a culture — namely, struggle to the death with other cultures. As a result, in the very act of strengthening a culture one emphasizes and even encourages the kind of activities which may lead to its destruction.

Will any culture eventually be affected by a mutation which will make its members interested in the survival of the human race? Can men be induced to work for the strength of humanity as a whole? There have been moves in that direction. To convince the individual that all men are brothers leads to a different kind of action "for the good of others." To argue that no man is an island and that the good of others necessarily affects his own good is a similar line. If any part of the human race eventually engineers a culture which powerfully supports activity for the sake of the human race, we may see new cultural designs of surprising power.

It would be a mistake, however, to try to justify them in any absolute sense. There is nothing fundamentally right about the survival of a culture, any more than there is something fundamentally right about the set of traits which define a species. Those who are induced by their culture to act in its service will do so, and the culture will benefit. They will not do so because of any certain knowledge in advance of where the culture is going. Those who want to know now what will be right in the future miss the whole point of evolution. Although we are now at the point at which we can design new mutations, by inventing new cultural practices, we do not know where other mutations will come from, nor can we surely predict their survival value. There is no way in which one can predict later stages in evolutionary history. It is not in the nature of evolution that this should be possible.

We do not even know what man will be like in the future simply as an organism. The processes of mutation and selection which have brought the species to the present point will continue, but of course, slowly. The process can be accelerated or retarded by changing the conditions under which members of the species survive and breed. If we can begin to change the genetic constitution of man, the process may be greatly accelerated.

Nor can we now tell what future cultures will be like. Those who work for the survival of their culture may solve fairly immediate problems and make reasonable guesses about a longer term. As our knowledge of human behavior improves, we shall no doubt design more effective practices and be able to induce the members of a culture to observe them. But many so-called mutations will be out of our control, as in the long run are the conditions of selection.

We shall work for the survival of our culture, if at all, because of the personal goods which are effective because of our genetic endowment, as these arise naturally or as part of our cultural environment. These are our values, and there are no alternatives. The culture will be strongest whose members are not deterred from acting in its interests by those who cite opposing values and claim a more imposing authority."[3]

----

3. From B. F. Skinner: A behavioral analysis of value judgments in the Biopsychology of Dev. ed. Ethel Tobach, Lester Aronson and Evelyn Shaw. Acad. Press, N.Y., 1971.

Assuming for a moment that survival value may be the only measuring rod against which all codes and value judgments must ultimately be tested, and that in itself may be a major point of controversy, the paradox of culture as a way of life and its perpetuation depends on the selection of such genetic traits that bring about behavior patterns of cooperation and mutual aid that are not at all uncommon among many animals. Reciprocally, the growth of civilization requires the suppression of such traits that promote cannibalism and the indiscriminate killing of members of their own species, a type of behavior which represents at best a blind alley in evolution but one which is excluded from the repertoire of practically all sucessfully adapting species.

For centuries, the dualistic view was accepted according to which culture, ethics, morality, law, order, manners, art, science and religion depend on a supreme heroic effort to conquer, control and counter the basic biological drives which tend to push each individual into the opposite direction. We are just discovering that this dualism of man's self-image is utter nonsense.

The cruelty, irrationality, violence, hatred, suspicion and the ceaseless sequence of killing, crusades, wars conquests and genocides are not as the naturalists have been telling us for so long the exclusive "natural" manifestation of an incompletely tamed animal flashing its teeth when challenged, but belong to a species, that although genetically most certainly not programmed to be angelic, includes in its behavioral repertoire along with considerable aggressiveness and preference for competition probably also a limited capacity for cooperation, mutual aid and even altruism. If left to his own devices, man would probably never have engaged in such excessive practice of cannibalism as he did, after he crossed the rubicon and became civilized.

114

VI

What follows from these considerations and speculations with respect to the question of the ethical implications of biology itself?

Granted that biology has no special insight as to what is to be considered good or evil or which ends are to be desirable and which to be condemned, it is, however, in a favored position to participate in the search to find the measures necessary to realize the genetic potential, which makes the realization of ethical programs possible, or to reject those social and ethical programs, which are completely out of accord with the genetic heritage of man. Thus, for example, a religion or ideology which insists on total celibacy would obviously be out of order, because it flagrantly contradicts the genetic potential of man as to be impracticable.

The mutual aid and subordination we so much admire in ants or bees may be ruled insufficient for homo sapiens. The attempt to impose the beehive pattern failed miserably in Sparta and in all subsequent civilizations which imitated Sparta, probably because the genetic endowment of man never adequately supported the kind of cooperation practiced in the beehive.

For the life sciences to be helpful in the search for desirable ethical and social programs, they must either learn to modify the genetic endowment itself, or enough information must be uncovered about the genetic program and the biological heritage that makes us "human" so as to enable us to formulate ethical programs that are realistic, possible, and in accord with human genetics. Both attempts are being pursued by the life sciences.

Genetic Utopias seek the roots of human imperfection in his inherited gene substance and suggest a road to "Paradise" through manipulation of that gene substance. They are perhaps the most ambitious of all Utopias ever proposed.

"Der Genetiker impliziert was Aufklaerer und Na-
turrechtler, Humanisten und Pschoanalytiker und So-
zialisten im Menschen bisher in rein vorwissenshaft-
licher Weise veraendern wollten, waehrend die Genetiker zum Kern vorgestossen sind, zu den Genen
es zu bewegen gilt, will man das Bild des Menschen
in dauerhafter Weise veraendern."[4]

Wolfgang Weiser in his "Die Genetische Utopie" stated the
case for the participation of the biologist to ethics like this:

"Die Schaetzungen uber die Geschwindigkeit mit der
wir den Verfall entgegen gehen schwanken betraecht-
lich, aber sowohl konservative wie radikale Specialis-
ten sind sich daruber einig, dass irgend etwas unter-
nommen werden muss, un die weithere Entwicklung
des Menschen lenkend zu beeinflussen."[4]

There is understandably both considerable excitement as
well as anxiety in anticipation of a future that will enable
man to manipulate his genetic material and thus influence the
evolutionary direction of his species. Conceptually, the problem
of how to control and alter the genetic substance itself, as
well as how to select and multiply specific genotypes in preference over others has already been solved in the laboratory.
Cloning, transplantation of nuclei into enucleated eggs, trans-
planting embryos to foster mothers and denying specific genetics
sites access to either transcription or translation of their message are methods which have been successfully tried in a
variety of organisms including viruses, bacteria, frogs and
rabbits. The application of these procedures to human populations is probably not quite as close at hand as some of the
crystal ball gazers would have us believe, but it will not be
beyond reach forever.

---

4. From W. Wieser, "Die Genetische Utopie," in Neue Deutsche
Haefte 1963.

Even if it were possible now to change the "gene pool" of human populations, we would not know at this stage of the game how to use that skill. We would be in the same boat as the blind man who, having just learned how to drive a car, does not know where to drive it to. The biologist is certainly not in a position to help or to give any directional signals on how to use the new knowledge for the common good because he is not equipped to judge which genotypes are desirable and which are not. To designate a gene as deleterious is a difficult if not impossible task, since we shall not know at any one time all the effects of a given gene under all sets of environments. Only in a few cases of overwhelming evidence, such as hemophilia, mongolism, Tay Sachs disease, will thoughtful biologists assume the risk of providing the label "deleterious" and suggest appropriate action.

Unless I read the future entirely wrong and much too conservatively, the transformation of the human species by permanent transformation of its gene pool will probably for some time to come occupy the minds of Sunday magazine writers rather than of serious biologists or genetic engineers. It is to be hoped that someone with the imagination of a Jules Verne will replace Isaac Azimov to show what could be done if we knew how. So, we shall probably be stuck with fitting our cultural programs to our genetic endowment, rather than to manipulate our genetic endowment to fit cultural aims and ambitions that are proposed by politicians, social scientists, reformers and human engineers. The life sciences can be of help in defining which of our ethical and cultural goals are genetically realistic and in phase with our biological heritage.

The question of whether man's genetic program is at all in accord with his cultural aims has taken on a new urgency in the light of the triple threat posed to the survival of all cultures by the distinct possibility of either mutual extinction through war or through overpopulation or destruction of the environment. The further evolution and survival of man as a culture-creating organism seems in doubt because at this stage of the game the survival of all forms and cultures seems to require total mobilization of a behavior for which man seems to have only a restricted biological endowment and very limited experience.

The most urgent question that is asked of the life sciences by those who are concerned with the human condition and are worried about the chances for man's survival is whether man is genetically capable of cooperation and collaboration and whether his preference for aggressive responses is really so irreversibly fixed in his genetic program that it cannot be blunted beyond what has been accomplished in spite of 5,000 years of civilization.

We shall return to an examination of this question in the following essay.

Aggression

I

There is not a generation alive today that does not remember war, murderous conflict, belligerent action, genocide or near genocide as part of their lives or the lives of their parents. It has touched them either as participants, victims or as shocked, frightened or numbed onlookers. The loaded question that is being asked from science is whether this bloody heritage is really the predestined consequence of man's nature. Translated into the more fashionable terms of modern communication language the question reads "Is man's genetic program for aggression so complete and so irrevocably fixed, that there exists no escape valve that might lend some meaning or credence to the dream of a future without war or without extinction?" The question is put far more eloquently by K. Lorenz in his book "On Aggression."

> "Let us imagine that an absolutely unbiased investigator on another planet, perhaps on Mars, is examining human behavior on earth, with the aid of a telescope whose magnification is too small to enable him to discern individuals and follow their separate behavior, but large enough for him to observe occurrences such as migrations of peoples, wars, and similar great historical events. He would never gain the impression that human behavior was dictated by intelligence, still less by responsible morality. If we suppose our extraneous observer to be a being of pure reason, devoid of instincts himself and unaware of the way in which all

instincts in general and aggression in particular can miscarry, he would be at a complete loss how to explain history at all. The ever-recurrent phenomena of history do not have reasonable causes. It is a mere commonplace to say that they are caused by what ccmmon parlance so aptly terms 'human nature.' Unreasoning and unreasonable human nature causes two nations to compete, though no economic necessity compels them to do so; it induces two political parties or religions with amazing similar programs of salvation to fight each other bitterly, and it impels an Alexander or a Napoleon to sacrifice millions of lives in his attempt to unite the world under his scepter. We have been taught to regard some of the persons who have committed these and similar absurdities with respect, even as 'great' men, we are wont to yield to the political wisdom of those in charge, and we are all so accustomed to these phenomena that most of us fail to realize how abjectly stupid and undesirable the historical mass behavior of humanity actually is.

Having realized this, however, we cannot escape the question why reasonable beings do behave so unreasonably. Undeniably, there must be superlatively strong factors which are able to overcome the commands of individual reason so completely and which are so obviously impervious to experience and learning. As Hegel said, 'What experience and history teach us is this — that people and governments never have learned anything from history, or acted on principles deduced from it.'

. . . Human behavior, and particularly human social behavior, far from being determined by reason and cultural tradition alone, is still subject to all the laws prevailing in all phylogenically adaptive instinctive behavior. Of these laws we possess a fair amount of knowledge from studying the instincts of animals. Indeed, if our extra-mundane observer were a knowledgeable ethologist, he would unavoidably draw the conclusion that man's social organization is very similar to those of rats, which, like humans, are social and peaceful beings within their clans, but veritable devils toward all fellow members of their species, not belonging to their own community. If, furthermore, our Martian naturalist knew of the explosive rise in human populations, the ever-increasing destructiveness of weapons, and the division of mankind into a few political camps, he would not expect the future of humanity to be more rosy than that of several hostile clans of rats on a ship almost devoid of food. And this prognosis would even be optimistic, for in the case of rats reproduction stops automatically when a certain state of overcrowding is reached while man as yet has no workable system for preventing the so-called population explosion. Furthermore, in the case of the rats, it is likely that after the wholesale slaughter enough individuals would be left over to propagate the species. In the case of man, this would not be so certain after the use of the hydrogen bomb."[1]

As religious or just as normal civilized human beings, we like to think that the violence we see erupting between any two angry fellowmen, or its counterpart, the carnage between races, religious groups or multiple alliances of nations, is a reflection not of man's true nature, but rather of a peculiar perversion of his makeup, and we would like science to reinforce this prejudice with good hard cash evidence.

1. From K. Lorenz "On Aggression," Harcourt Brace & World Inc., New York, 1967.

Classical Darwinian biology has challenged such self-righteous, semi-religious notions and has suggested that all the amazing paradoxes of man's unreasonable and seemingly inhuman actions fall into place like pieces of a jigsaw puzzle once we admit that *aggression* is part of the program of all animal life or that it is a sort of universal law of the animal kingdom. This somewhat simplistic view has of course long been superseded by more sophisticated analyses of the biological basis of aggression, but old myths are slow to die and they often have greater power to sway men into action than the rarified insights accessible only to scholars.

To paraphrase Medawar:

> "All these so-called 'biological judgments' were bad judgments, based on bad biology, or more likely on misunderstanding of anything that reputable biologists have ever proclaimed about the operational forces guiding man's origin, his heritage, and his place in the natural order of evolution."[2]

Fighting obviously occurs so widely in the animal kingdom that it cannot be dismissed as accidental or abnormal. In reality, aggressive behavior is a common and apparently useful part of the daily lives of many but not all animals and only rarely does it become destructive or harmful. What has also been demonstrated, however, is that *some* animals have evolved alternatives to aggression in responding to those challenges and stimuli that normally elicit adaptively adequate aggressive responses.

The question that really matters to man in his quest to discover himself is whether the so familiar aggressive behavior, which he recognized in himself and his fellow men, is the

------

2. Peter Medawar, "The Future of Man." Basic Books, N.Y., 1959.

universal response of *all* living creatures to real or imaginary threats to their existence or whether it is merely a perversion of human nature. Obviously nature is not so stereotyped that the same response pattern to similar or identical challenges is imprinted and fixed into the program of *every* living species.

The primates who compose the group to which man belongs, show a considerable range in aggressiveness from the gibbon in which both sexes fight so vigorously that they can exist only in small family groups, to the howling monkeys whose fighting almost never goes beyond vocalization in either sex. As for man, there is no doubt that he ranks high in the scale of primate aggressiveness.

K. Lorenz has pointed out that in all primates, interspecific as well as the more rarely practiced intraspecific, fighting behavior indeed serves a number of biologically respectable objectives, mainly coincident with the survival of the species.

"Darwin had already raised the question of the survival value of fighting, and he has given us an enlightening answer: It is always favorable to the future of a species if the stronger of the two rivals takes possession either of the territory or of the desired female. As so often, this truth of yesterday is not the untruth of today but only a special case; ecologists have recently demonstrated a much more essential function of aggression. Ecology — derived from the Greek oikos, the house — is the branch of biology that deals with the manifold reciprocal relations of the organism to its natural surroundings — its 'household' — which of course includes all other animals and plants native to the environment. Unless the special interests of a social organization demand close aggregation of its members, it is obviously most expedient to spread the individuals of an animal species as evenly as possible over the available habitat. To use a human analogy, if, in a certain area, a larger number of doctors, builders, and mechanics want to exist, the representatives of these professions will do well to settle as far away from each other as possible. The danger of too dense a population of an animal species settling in one part of the available biotope and exhausting all its sources of nutrition and so starving can be obviated by a mutual repulsion acting on the animals of the same species, effecting their regular spacing out, in much the same manner as electrical charges are regularly distributed all over the surface of a spherical conductor. This, in plain terms, is the most important survival value of intra-specific aggression."[3]

It may indeed be favorable for the survival of the species if the stronger takes possession or ultimately just survives, but the final attainment of such an objective would be arriving at the absurd; since the stronger will, in turn, become the weaker until there is only one survivor left. Such an arrangement will ultimately mean death rather than survival for the species.

"We must try to step outside our groups and gaze down to the battlefields of the human animal with the unbiased eye of a hovering Martian. It is not going to be easy, and I want to make it clear at the outset that nothing I say should be constructed as implying that I am favouring one group against another, or suggesting that one group is inevitably superior to another.

"Using a harsh evolutionary argument, it might be suggested that if two human groups clash and one exterminates the other, the winner is biologically more successful than the other. But if we view the species

---

3. From Konrad Lorenz, "On Aggression," Harcourt, Brace & World, Inc., New York, 1967.

as a whole this argument no longer applies. It is a small view. The bigger view is that if we had contrived to live competitively but peacefully alongside one another, the species as a whole would be that much more successful.

"It is this large view that we must try to take. If it seems an obvious one, then we have some rather difficult explaining to do. We are not a mass-spawning species like certain kinds of fish that produce thousands of young in one go, most of which are doomed to be wasted and only a few survive. We are not quantity breeders, we are quality breeders, producing a few offspring, lavishing more care and attention on them and looking after them for a longer period than any other animal. After devoting nearly two decades of parental energy to them it is, apart from anything else, grotesquely inefficient to send them off to be knifed, shot, burned and bombed by the offspring of other men. Yet, in little more than a single century (from 1820 to 1945). no less than 49 million human beings were killed in inter-group clashes of one sort or another. This is the difficult explaining we have to do, if it is so obvious to the human intellect that it would be better to live peacefully. We describe killings as men 'behaving like animals,' but if we could find a wild animal that showed signs of acting in this way, it would be more precise to describe it as behaving like men. The fact is that we cannot find such a creature. We are dealing with another of the dubious properties that make modern man a unique species."[4]

_____

4. Desmond Morris, "The Human Zoo," McGraw Hill Comp.

Whether or not there is some internal need for aggression as there is for eating or sex is a question which has not been clearly answered. I venture the guess that a behavior pattern that was initially invented to assure the survival of the species must do so by providing some deep and continuing satisfaction to the individual organism also. Just like reproductive behavior assures propagation of the species by giving release to the libido of the individual members of the population, so aggression probably became so firmly established as a way of life of the group by satisfying the need for release of frustration by its members. Aggression is probably for relief of tension what sex is for the release of libido. Both provide tremendous satisfaction to the individual and because of this, they serve as major mechanisms for the survival of the species.

According to clinical experience, the two most common reactions to an unbearable situation are to fight it or to try to escape from it in some way. Scott cites the example of 'a teen-age boy who goes to a dance with a girl and very much enjoys her company as well as the intimate physical contact of dancing. Later she repulses his more ardent advances, and he responds with angry words and tells her that she is a cold-hearted, teasing witch, or words to that effect. She says she never wants to see him again, and marches into the house.' Here is a case where aggression seems to be useless, or, as the boy would put it, telling her off was the wrong approach. It is also an example of a very common phenomenon among members of our society, that of frustration leading to aggression. . . . Sometimes this results in a sort of chain reaction, as when a man is reprimanded by his boss, gets cross with his wife, who needlessly spanks her little boy, who picks a fight with his brother, where at last the aggression can be expressed in both directions. In the whole series of reactions, none of the behavior has anything to do with the original stimulus, and hence it all seems to be maladaptive."

But was this behavior really so useless?

". . . The boy who quarreled with the girl who frustrated

him had at least driven her away so that she will not frustrate him again. The man who takes out his exasperation on his wife has not done anything about the relationship with his boss, but he has at least relieved some of his feelings. However, this brings up the problem of the human situations in which a person could make a better adaptation and does not do so. Sometimes the chosen attempt at adaptation may actually make the situation worse than it originally was. For example, if a man takes out his aggressive feelings on his wife too often, she may eventually retaliate, with the result that he has a bad time at home as well as a bad time at work."[5]

But inference, the somewhat simplistic conclusion offers itself that the only, if not the easiest, way to remove "aggression" from the repertoire of human behavior is to create conditions for man that will either eliminate or at least minimize the chances of experiencing frustration. That is exactly the premise upon which so many Utopias of the sociologists and the social planners, past and present, were constructed. They reason that only by minimizing the factors that cause frustration can one hope to reduce possible aggressive confrontation between human groups, races, nations and classes.

One may legitimately argue whether freedom from frustration provided by a social order in which all frustration-provoking conditions are removed from man's experiences is not too ambitious a project, and also whether it is not too high a price to pay — assuming, rightly or wrongly, that some of the best products of human culture were born or at least invented following exposure to frustration.

In any case, the chance of establishing a social order this side of Heaven in which all conditions that normally provoke frustration in the individual are successfully and completely eliminated are so dim as to be almost negligible. To insulate man from all the adversities with which he cannot immediately cope would require the building of a world akin to a huge air

_____

5. From J. P. Scott, "Aggression." Chicago Univ. Press, 1958.

and moisture conditioned, sterile hothouse; life in such an environment would probably be the greatest of all frustrations.

Implicit in any social program, Utopian blueprint, or any plan, that may call for action to change man's relationship to man, is of course the presupposition that not only the environment but that within limits man can be changed and/or modified, or in more poetic terms, that man an be good, is inherently good or that his goodness can be freed and realized. It is the examination of this premise toward which science, particularly the life sciences, can profitably contribute.

"Nature," so Lorenz teaches us, has hit upon two reliable measures to protect species of sociable animals from the danger of self-annihilation by putting severe constraints on the effectiveness of "infighting." According to Lorenz, offensive weapons at the disposal of most animals are 1) either insufficient to injure or kill members of their own species, or 2) those animals that have that capacity to kill members of their own lack the "nerve" to do so. Lorenz cites as an example of the former the dove or the hare or the chimpanzee, each of which is incapable of knocking out their fellow member with one bite or one blow, unlike the raven which can peck out the eye of another with one thrust of its beak, or a wolf that can rip another with one single bite. In contrast, all those species that actually are capable of killing living members of their own kind swiftly and rapidly, have an inhibitory mechanism built into them, that prevents their members from going haywire in their rage, thus assuring that their numbers will never be depleted below a critical point. One of the more widespread mechanisms which prevents self-destruction of species is the emotion of pity or something akin to it that can be aroused in the aggressive animal by the victim. This has been demonstrated by a simple experiment described by Scott.

> "If we take an experienced male mouse and subject
> him to the attacks of a trained fighter, he will be

strongly stimulated to fight. We can prevent his escape by putting the two mice together in a cage. Adaptation is difficult because the inexperienced fighter is outmatched by the trained animal.

"The results are simple and clear-cut. At first the experienced mouse tries to fight back, and the two tumble over and over, biting and scratching. However, the fighter is more effective in hurting his opponent, who begins to run away. If he were not confined, the losing mouse could escape from the victor completely a successful adaptation. Since this first form of adaptation did not work and he cannot get away, he soon shows another type of behavior. As soon as attacked, he leaps away and stands still, holding out his forepaws toward the attacker. This is a passive defensive attitude, and as we watch we see that it has the effect of holding off the aggressor. It is also less stimulating, since the aggressor no longer gets hurt. As a result, the attacks gradually let up until the attacker is apparently satisfied with merely threatening the losing mouse, who immediately stiffens in a defensive attitude. If we confine the animals still more and let them fight in a narrow passage where the losing mouse cannot stand up, he simply lies down flat and makes no movement whatsoever. He has become completely passive and is apparently not adapting to the situation at all, but this very passivity is less stimulating to the attacking mouse, so that the victim takes less punishment in the long run. In short, the mouse seems to do the best thing possible under the circumstances."[6]

---

6. From J. P. Scott, "Aggression." Chicago Univ. Press, 1958.

The situation described in the laboratory mouse is duplicated in nature:

"There are built-in safety devices which prevent professional carnivores from abusing their killing power to destroy fellow members of their own species. A lion or a wolf may, on extremely rare occasions, kill another by one angry stroke, but . . . all heavily armed carnivores possess sufficiently reliable inhibitions which prevent the self-destruction of the species.

"In human evolution, no inhibitory mechanisms preventing sudden manslaughters were initially necessary because quick killing was impossible anyhow. No selection pressure arose in the prehistory of mankind to breed inhibitory mechanisms preventing the killing of conspecifics until, all of a sudden, the invention of artificial weapons upset the equilibrium of killing potential and social inhibitions. When it did, man's position was very nearly that of a dove which, by some unnatural trick of nature, had suddenly acquired the beak of a raven. . . . Inhibitions controlling aggression in various social animals, preventing it from injuring or killing fellow members of the species are most important and consequently most highly differentiated in those animals which are capable of killing living creatures of about their own size. A raven can peck out the eye of another with one thrust of its beak, a wolf can rip the jugular vein of another with a single bite. There would be no more ravens and no more wolves if reliable inhibitions did not prevent such actions. Neither a dove nor a hare nor even a chimpanzee is able to kill its own kind with a single peck or bite. Since there rarely is, in nature, the possibility of such an animal's seriously injuring one of its own kind, there is no selection pressure at work here to breed 'in-killing' inhibitions. The absence of such inhibitions is apparent to the animal keeper, to his own and to his animals' disadvantage, if he does not take seriously the intra-specific fight of completely 'harmless' animals. Under the unnatural conditions of captivity, where a defeated animal cannot escape from its victor, it may be killed slowly and cruelly."[7]

The human predicament may be twice compounded, however. Our ancestors may have become transformed too quickly into ravens, without giving them time to evolve inhibitory mechanisms that would prevent fratricide. In this respect, human are "Johnny come latelys." At the present juncture when humanity, or at least a sizable portion of it, had reached a plateau of compassion and pity and attained a limited reluctance to kill indiscriminately, new weapons have been invented which so effectively screen the killer against the stimulus which would normally arouse his pity and mobilize his killing inhibition, that there is a chance not altogether remote, that extinction by self-destruction may for the first time be accomplished, by, of all species, civilized man.

"If moral responsibility and unwillingness to kill have indubitably increased, the ease and emotional impunity of killing have increased at the same rate. The distance at which all shooting weapons take effect screens the killer against the stimulus situation which would otherwise activate his killing inhibitions. The deep emotional layers of our personality simply do not register the fact that the crooking of the forefinger to release a shot tears the entrails of an-

---

7. From K. Lorenz, "On Aggression." Harcourt Brace and World, N.Y., 1967.

other man. No sane man would even go rabbit hunting for pleasure if the necessity of killing his prey with his natural weapons brought home to him the full, emotional realization of what he is actually doing.

"The same principle applies, to an even greater degree, to the use of modern remote control weapons. The man who presses the releasing button is so completely screened against seeing, hearing, or otherwise emotionally realizing the consequences of his action, that he can commit it with impunity — even if he is burdened with the power of imagination. Only thus can it be explained that perfectly good-natured men who would not even smack a naughty child, proved to be perfectly able to release rockets or to lay carpets of incendiary bombs on sleeping cities, thereby comitting hundreds and thousands of children to a horrible death in the flames. The fact that good normal men did this, is as eerie as any fiendish atrocity of war!"[8]

Aggression, as K. Lorenz has pointed out, may be a useful form of behavior insofar as it assures the survival of a species in an ecological biosphere that is too small or too meager to support populations that have multiplied to excessive numbers. Aggression may indeed shield a species from the danger of extinction by population pressure in an ecological niche that can feed and support only a limited number, but it accomplishes this trick by only the thinnest of margins. Aggression is at best a dangerous tool in the battle for survival of a species.

It would certainly add to the wisdom of nature and be in line with the way "she" solves similar problems — if a hypothetical "biostat" functioning very much in the manner a

----

8. From K. Lorenz, "On Aggression." Harcourt Brace and World, N.Y., 1967.

thermostat would operate in the system, capable of switching behavior patterns and attitudes among the members of a species, so that whenever the number of a socially interacting group, tribe or pack might reach a critical low dangerpoint, competition and rivalry among its members, would be curbed. Depending upon need, a species could quickly switch from aggressive behavior to cooperation and in this way assure survival of the population in an ever-changing environment. The existence of such a workable biostat would require of course a genetically built-in neural circuitry that makes possible a type of behavior pattern that we recognize as "intelligent cooperation."

What are the implications of all this for the human situation? Aggression as an adaptive effort when judged strictly on such biological criteria as survival of individuals or population is not always successful, since one of its effects is to stimulate the opponent to fight back and the attacker may lose. In many situations, aggression is adaptive only to the winner, a point which is obvious. As the risks for survival through attack are amplified, aggression for the human species has lost its last vestige of adaptive value and has become strictly maladaptive.

Doubts about aggression and uneasiness about the threat which unrestricted infighting may pose to the survival and welfare of any and all human groups are as old as civilization itself. In fact, the history of civilization since its dawn has been marked by a certain ambivalence. Some of our cultural ancestors, particularly those pictured in the sagas of the Norse and Teutonic tribes, and in the epics of the ancient Persians, Hebrews, Greeks and Romans, give assent to ideals in which fighting and individual bravery played a strong part and applause was reserved for the successful and resourceful attacker. These sentiments were tempered by the Ten Commandments, the Prophets, the Sermon on the Mount and the eloquent longing for the City of God and the universal brotherhood of Man that is also part of Western and probably of all civilization. Western man, while exulting Alexander, Caesar and Napoleon and all the heroes who killed so well, never quite let go of Christ and the Prophets.

"Our present cultural ideals are in a state of transition and as in most complex societies they are not entirely consistent with each other. A well-brought-up boy in our society is taught that he must be aggressive in order to succeed in life. Whether his adult models are salesmen or statesmen, he learns that aggressiveness is a good thing and leads to success. At the same time, he is taught that aggression is a bad thing and that he must not start fights or pick on other people. His religious training may go even farther and state that even the feelings concerned with aggression are a bad thing. The result is a cultural ideal which is often difficult to live up to and creates many special problems. For the small boy who must not fight unless attacked, it means that he is automatically at a great disadvantage in any fight into which he is forced. For the adult, it may mean constant stimulation from his aggressive fellows, without opportunity to fight back or even to express anger. The result is likely to be some of the psychosomatic ailments or simply that many individuals seek out social positions which do not require this constant strain."[9]

Incidentally, this ambivalence is by no means restricted to Western societies. We tend to think of the Indian tribes of North America as being bloodthirsty and aggressive, but among them are the Hopi who call themselves the "peaceful people." A Hopi is not even supposed to have angry thoughts toward anyone and is seriously upset if he does. Mead (1954)

---

9. From J. P. Scott, "Aggression." Chicago Univ. Pren, 1958.

has shown that among the Arapese tribes the ideal behavior for both sexes is peacefulness and non-aggression. Warfare, known to be an almost universal occupation of all people since the beginning of recorded history and probably before, is, strangely enough absent among the Australian aborigines and the Eskimos. Whether or not the absence of warfare among these people is related to the fact that they lived in an extremely unfavorable environment, or that their societies were too small or too far apart to make warfare possible, as Scott suggests, is difficult to assess. Obviously, in a society whose membership is so small that it approaches a critical margin and which inhabits an environment so austere and unfavorable as to seriously threaten survival, warfare with its inherent risk of reducing the population even further below the critical safety point, would not be remotely profitable. Against such odds, "intelligent cooperation" may be the only alternative to extinction. The risks may, of course, be equally great to an overpopulated society squeezed on a tight little island; a situation that is rapidly approached by the whole human species inhabiting this planet. Here too, "intelligent cooperation" may be the only alternative to extinction.

The troubling question remains: Are we biologically equipped to lend a hand to our own evolution and increase the odds in favor of our own survival by replacing long ingrained response patterns of asserting ourselves by attack, whenever we think we are threatened and wherever we think we can win, with another arrangement of behavior that includes peaceful cooperation, compromise, toleration, and postponement, if not outright abolition, of conflict?

Upon surveying the over 50,000 year old experience of man, one can't help thinking that we simply are not programmed for a course of peaceful cooperation with our fellow species members. But suppose man is not programmed rigidly at all. Let us suppose for a moment that the end product of vertebrate evolution is a nervous system with such an excess of circuits so that only a fraction of those circuits that are structurally available, can be utilized in the lifespan of any single member of the species. A selection of those circuits that are to be operative out of the many that are available to the organism will have to be made sometime in the life history of the organism. Unlike other features of the organism, such as its structure, physiological mechanism, or biochemical profile, all of which are differentiated very early during ontogeny in the relative isolation of prenatal life, the decisions which specify the nervous system may be made somewhat later in life while encountering the first outside experiences. It is then that presumably the choices could be made that determine which of the infinite number of neural circuits are to be connected and which are to remain silent or inoperative.

The evidence accumulated during the last 25 years by neurobiologists clearly demonstrates that the central nervous system can be and is modified in accordance with the quantity and quality of outside experience. Brain size, volume, and surface area, number of synapses, number of neurons, number of dendritic branching, RNA turnover, concentration of selective brain enzymes and transmitter substances all have been shown to be influenced by environmental stimulation and early experience. Experiments in which an enriched environment was provided to the embryonic animal during early nervous system development attest to the permanent modification of the nervous system. In a nervous system containing approximately 4 billion nerve cells, there must exist an almost infinite number of neural circuits ready to be connected by the appropriate outside signals, and the number of available circuits may well reach infinity. The evolution of the vertebrate nervous system points to just such an excess in the supply of available nerve cell connections.

The study of the phylogeny of the vertebrate nervous system teaches us that practically no component of the brain of earlier more primitive ancestral vertebrates has been discarded in evolution. The amphibian brain is built on top of the fish brain; the reptilian brain is added on, and the mammalian brain is superimposed over all the other ancestral structures. Assuming for a moment that primates and man present the end of the line of this tract of evolution, "Man" may be born with a circuitry so vast as to permit a repertoire of behavior that can be switched advantageously to fit any conceivable change in an ever-changing environment.

There is some precedent for a similar kind of extravagance in evolution. According to the modern theory of antibody formation (Burnet McFarlane) we are told that the vertebrate animal is already born with vast reservoirs of antibodies long before it is exposed to foreign antigens. The organism at birth has available molecules against any conceivable foreign protein including viruses, bacteria and pathogens with which it may ever come into contact during its lifetime and also against those which it probably will never encounter. These antibody molecules are locked away in cells that collectively form a kind of chemical memory. Only the actual encounter with a given set of foreign proteins, as for example, during infection, will stimulate the cells containing the relevant memory to respond by either replicating or discharging more of its stored product into the blood stream and thus fill each organism's special antibody titer in accordance with the antigenic challenges facing it during its lifetime. The parallel to the nervous system is obvious. All the circuits are there; — which ones are to be connected depends on the kind of experiences impinging on a young, plastic developing nervous system. The first clue of the powerful, nay, traumatic push which early experience exerts on the direction into which the young nervous system is specified came from observations on mate selection in chicks and ducks. Briefly, the gist of these observations has been that the choice of the mate by adult birds seems to be related to the nature of the object to which the newly hatched bird directed its first response shortly after emerging from the egg shell. This phenomena is generally referred to in the scientific literature as *imprinting*.

The evidence from the neuroscience suggests that maximum modifiability of the central nervous system may take place very early in life. The older assumption that imprinting must be completed within a very limited "critical period" of CNS maturation has since been questioned; although once the sensitive period is over, strange objects elicit withdrawal rather than approach. In any case, exposure to objects, even in later life, can modify preferences. According to the more recent view (see Hinde in Biopsychology of Development, ed. E. Tobach)[10] imprinting becomes not a sudden irreversible all or none process, but something much more flexible, success of which depends on a great number of variables.

The selection of the circuitry depends on the imprinting process which in turn is influenced and directed by the experiences that are made available during critical periods of brain differentiation. Possibly, in humans, the whole lifetime may constitute "a critical period" during which a nervous system as long as it remains relatively plastic, can be imprinted.

Those of us who put our trust in education as a major tool for the betterment of man, ought not to ignore the lessons to be learned from "imprinting in animals" and the significance of the "early critical period." In fact, we ought to take courage from it. Education and training would not be possible unless some measure of permanent modification can be imposed on the central nervous system or those of its components that are responsible for a particular type of behavior.

Religion, socialism, democracy, psychoanalysis, all the levers that have been suggested for liberating man to unselfish "goodness" are based on faith in the educability of man. The partial success of and the powerful hold that each of these attempts has held over large numbers of the human population itself points to an often overlooked biological fact, namely,

----

10. R. A. Hinde, 1971. "Some Problems in the Study of the Development of Social Behavior."

the modifiability of the central nervous system. Education may possibly be defined as nothing less than CNS modification.

The search for the genetic heritage of man, so vigorously pursued by anthropologists, zoologists, geneticists, psychologists and social critics in their efforts to understand civilized man's difficulties and dilemmas by identifying his primitive heritage may turn out to be a chase after phantoms.

Man's brain may be the least rigidly programmed of all the primates. As happens so often, the scientists discover, with great fanfare, the obvious and translate into their own jargon what ordinary people learn by a kind of life experience osmosis. Chances are that any farmer without benefit of genetics can confirm that a puppy can turn into a vicious mutt if it is raised on an emotional starvation diet, and its twin can turn into the most loyal and lovable "Lassie" if it is given an excess of love, care attention and cuddling.

If a child lives with intimidation, he learns to be shy.

If a child lives with distrust, he learns to be deceitful.

If a child lives with antagonism, he learns to be hostile.

If a child lives with ridicule, he learns to be timid.

If a child lives with shame, he learns to feel guilt.

If a child lives with domination, he learns to be resigned.

If a child lives with scorn, he learns to be bitter.

If a child lives with affection, he learns to love.

If a child lives with encouragement, he learns to be confident.

If a child lives with truth, he learns to be just.

If a child lives with praise, he learns to appreciate.

If a child lives with sharing, he learns to be considerate.

If a child lives with knowledge, he learns to be wise.

If a child lives with patience, he learns to be tolerant.

If a child lives with approval, he learns to like himself.

If a child lives with sensitivity, he learns to be understanding.

If a child lives with happiness, he will find love and beauty.

139

Roots of Religion

I

In the preceding chapters, I have tried to present some of the quintessence of the ideas and hopes as I understood them, that were expressed and sharpened in conversation and debates among both young and older inhabitants of an urban college campus during the last troubled decade.

In this last and final chapter, I should like to attempt to present some of the ideas derived from the encounters with religion that sustained and nourished the humanist mood.

The real concentrated efforts to search for the precepts of religion were linked, initially at least, to the movement of *"Conscientious Objection."* Conscientious objection was never organized into a joint strategy but therein lay its great appeal. Conscientious objection was an intensely personal response to a very real dilemma of universal proportions. So spontaneous and so wide-spread and so similar was the intellectual route which propelled men to become conscientious objectors, that it deserves to be called a movement.

To a generation suspicious of doctrine, distrustful of ideology and fearful of organized strategy, in pursuit of universal goals, conscientious objection became almost a joyful exercise because of the hope it engendered that an intensely personal act of conscience, if practiced by enough men of like mind, yet acting as individuals "doing their thing," could conceivably make a difference in the real world so that "suppose they gave a war and nobody came," instead of being an exercise in the "absurd," might become a distinct possibility.

"Conscientious objection, while not as visible as a protest march on Washington, D.C., is in many ways more effective, because it is a lasting protest. The decision to become a CO, or to go to prison for one's beliefs, is a decision one lives with the rest of one's life. Indeed, it influences the direction of one's life. It's a little like a conversion to Christianity: one is not born a Christian, or a conscientious objector; rather, there comes a time when it is necessary to make the difficult and conscientious decision to try to make one's whole life reflect his beliefs.

"To me the most important ones who will be touched by such an act of living protest are our own sons and daughters, perhaps still unborn. Each generation learns its values from those who go on before. By choosing not to go to war, the CO sets for his children an example of positive choice and worshipful initiative that will help their generation break from the mad tradition of war.

"For them, a CO can be a very potent witness, teaching them to live according to their beliefs, encouraging them to become aware of the implications and possibilities involved in every choice they make. For they will see not a single act of protest, but a whole life of conviction that will help them be 'doers of the word, and not hearers only' (James 1:22)."[1]

---

1. From David Brunet's "Response," Event Magazine, 1971, published by American Lutheran Church. David Brunet is a Lutheran CO. He graduated from St. Olaf College in 1969 and is currently a graduate student in English at Columbia University. (This article was secured through the assistance of Lutheran Selective Service Information, an office of the Lutheran Council/YSA, 315 Park Avenue South, New York, N.Y. 10010).

Those Americans "selected" by their government to participate in an enterprise requiring them to kill were faced relatively early in their lives with an acid test of their convictions. For guidance, they frequently had to turn to their early forgotten contact with religion to help them explain to themselves and to others the reason for their refusal to fight and/or to kill. The majority who chose that route had about as much time as their 2S deferment allotted them to brush up on their religion and come up with a convincing answer. When they attempted to recall the concepts of earlier religious training and tried to formulate their own objection to killing, precious little help was forthcoming from organized religion to reconcile the secular challenge with the word of God. Unfortunately, most religious congregations, with the one shining exception of the Quakers, failed to give guidance on what to do when religious tenets become incompatible with the obligations that were thrust upon them by the state. There may be excuse for such reluctance in tyrannical or oppressive societies. In America, however, where, thanks to a long and enthusiastic tradition of democracy, methods have been evolved for the orderly change of laws that are either unwise or unjust, and alternatives have been offered to exempt individuals from obligations that are generally imposed on the rest of the population if they clearly offend his religious· and moral precepts, there was little excuse for such procrastination.

It is probably grossly unfair and an oversimplification to equate with cowardice the reluctance by churches and synagogues alike to participate at least in the consideration of this problem or to proclaim conscientious objection as the only logical position compatible with religious doctrine. But this is the somewhat rash judgment of many of the present-day generation of young Americans, quite a few of whom felt cynically abandoned by their rabbis and priests when they needed them most. But oversimplification and erroneous judgments have a power of their own to sway people and influence action. Much of the apathy and discontent of young people in organized religion is based on the presumption that religion is irrelevant in today's world precisely because religious leaders refused to take a stand at a time when the most sensitive moral issue had to be faced by them alone. They preferred to concentrate instead on such problems as the propriety of mixed marriages or the sanctity of prenatal life, rather than that of post-natal life. In defense of the Catholic Church, it must be said that it has produced the Berrigans and Father Goppi and Sister Elizabeth, and their followers. There are fewer on the Protestant scene and no comparable Berrigans emerged from the ranks of the Jewish rabbis.

Imagine what might have happened if religious leaders of all denominations all over the land had joined in a proclamation stating that active participation in war, and certainly the one engaged in by the United States in Vietnam, is clearly in violation of the explicit commandments made repeatedly in both the Old and New Testament and that, therefore, every believing Christian and Jew who accepts either the so-called "Old Testament" or the "New Testament" as a fundamental guide for his moral and ethical action must, when called upon to participate in war, make a choice of either revoking or upholding his or her religious convictions. If he chooses to uphold his religion, he must refuse to take part in the fight and seek to be excused. He cannot have it both ways. The Catholic Church had the power to excommunicate which it has used for lesser sins. Even a proclamation that participation in the war is in contempt of religion and in violation of several of the most sacred religious commandments held by both Christians and Jews alike would have put an end to the silly exercise whereby young boys, by nature untrained in the articulation of their convictions, had to engage unaided and without "benefit of clergy" in arguments with Draft and Appeals Boards which usually were composed of men who were totally unqualified to judge theological doctrine and philosophical arguments of ethics. So the kids stood alone and battled as best as they could with their conscience. Jesus Christ may be their superstar *now,* but few go to church to see him perform there.

The turn toward religion may have originally started simply because the laws in America were written in such a way as to favor religious conviction over philosophical or sociological ones in the granting of "conscientious objector" status. The latest Supreme Court decision notwithstanding, almost all conscientious objectors sooner or later turned to religion and found there the sustenance to explain to themselves and to others the reason for their refusal to make war.

The a priori maxim which is shared by Quakers, Catholics, Jews, Lutherans, Episcopalians and, yes, Agnostics and Atheists is the admittedly irrational faith that (1) there exists an absolute injunction against killing one's fellow man and against causing him unnecessary suffering, (2) that this injunction is imposed from above, and (3) that there is no appeal from it. Those who could identify the source of that injunction as a very personal God were prepared to renew their allegiance to Him. For others, it was not quite so simple and they were off on an odyssey into theology. From these efforts, considerable fallout came that stimulated revival of religious feeling and sensitivity for religious faith far and above the objectives in search of which the excursion into religion and theology was initially undertaken.

I think that it is important to review the encounter with religion into which so many people were propelled by the choices that the war and the draft imposed upon them, in spite of the fact that both of these factors which cast their shadows over their lives for so long have happily been removed now.

The fact that the war is over now and the draft abolished makes a review of the soul-reaching argument not less important, but rather more so, than it was only a few years ago, when these facts of life caused sleepless nights and nightmares to draft-aged sons and their parents. Fortunately and hopefully, the passions are slowly subsiding, but the dilemma of the two allegiances shall surely continue to be with us.

In the following pages, I would like to present some of the attempts at amateur theology and try not to interject myself or my own interpretations. That such objectivity is not entirely posible, I readily admit. The very selection of passages from a rather voluminous literature hidden away in the Selective Service Law Review and Draft Board files reflects nothing more than my own prejudice as to which arguments appeal to me as either eloquent or relevant or both.

The essays in the succeeding pages were written in reply to a routine questionnaire handed out by Selective Service Boards to anyone who wished to claim conscientious objector status. Unintentionally, no doubt they provoked the greatest outpouring of layman theology since the Reformation and in no small way contributed to what is fashionably sometimes referred to as the religious revival in America.

II

The form which had to be answered is reproduced below. Essentially each prospective conscientious objector had to address himself to four questions.

SPECIAL FORM FOR CONSCIENTIOUS OBJECTOR

The purpose of this questionnaire is to assist your local board in determining whether you qualify for classification as a conscientious objector. Before you answer the questions you may wish to read the pamphlet, "Conscientious Objector," which is available at your local board office.

Print or type, on separate sheets of paper, a statement answering the questions below. Sign both your statement and this form. Attach your statement to the form and mail or deliver them to your local board.

To be classified as a conscientious objector you must be opposed to war in any form. Your objection must be based on moral or ethical beliefs, or beliefs which are commonly accepted as religious. Your beliefs must influence your life as the belief in God influences the life of one who is a traditionally religious conscientious objector. To qualify, your conscience must be spurred by deeply held moral, ethical or religious beliefs which would give you no peace if you allowed yourself to become a combatant member of the armed forces.

Include in your statement, if possible, responses to the following. If you wish you may attach letters of reference from persons who know you or any other information you would like to bring to the attention of your local board.

1. Describe the beliefs which are the basis for your claim for classification as a conscientious objector.

2. Will your beliefs permit you to serve in a position in the armed forces where the use of weapons is not required? If not, why?

3. Explain how you acquired the beliefs which are the basis of your claim. Your answer may include such information as the influence of family members or other persons; religious training if applicable; experiences at school; membership in organizations; books and readings which influenced you. You may wish to provide any other information which will help in explaining why you believe as you do.

4. Explain what most clearly shows that your beliefs are deeply held.

5. Do your beliefs affect the way you live? Describe how your beliefs affect the type of work you will do to earn a living or the types of activity you participate in during nonworking hours?

6. Describe any specific actions or incidents of your life that show you believe as you do.

Insure your signature is on the reverse side and all information requested is complete.

STATEMENT IN REPLY TO SELECTIVE SERVICE FORM 150

By: *An Anonymous Objector*

1. Describe the beliefs which are the basis for your claim for classification as a conscientious objector.

    I just couldn't kill anybody. I don't want to kill anybody. It is against my religion. It is against the will of God. I couldn't kill any of my brothers. There would not be life on earth if people always fight and kill. I don't think any war is meant to be. Here in the States if you get in a fight they put you in jail, in the military they put you in slavery to kill another guy. I couldn't see doing it. I don't think God would want me to kill others and have others kill me.

2. Will your beliefs permit you to serve in a position in the armed forces where the use of weapons is not re-required? If not, why?

    It's still the same thing, it all contributes to war anyway you put it. By being a Medic, I would be participating in war.

3. Explain how you acquired the beliefs which are the basis of your claim.

    I never fought at home or school. I get along good with my friends most of the time. When I was younger we never had any guns in the house. I never owned a gun. I never went hunting. I never liked to watch war movies. When I was about six years old

I started to go to church regularly. I went to Sunday School. I learned about God. I learned how to love one another and to have peace on earth. My parents went to a Baptist Church quite often. I have a half brother who is an active Catholic. He never misses church. Every Sunday he goes to church. He has been going ever since he was very little. My little brother went to a Baptist Church for a while then he got me to go and then he got my folks to go.

At age 18 I can't say I objected to military service but I did not know anything about conscientious objection. My friends influenced me a little. My friend Dave served in Viet Nam and told me what it was like. It made me feel down on war. He is the one who told me I should see a draft counselor. I received an induction order. I was scared. I was not expecting it. I could not accept it. I just could not accept going to war or having anything to do with Selective Service. I went to see a counselor. I went to see the Reverend. He informed me about my rights as a conscientious objector and told me how to get the conscientious objector form. Now I realize I can't kill anybody so I have filed as a conscientious objector.

4. Explain what most clearly shows that your beliefs are deeply held.

I am not an outgoing person, therefore I have not said much to others about my feelings toward war or any form of military service. I have discussed my feelings about war with my parents. I have expressed my feelings extensively with my counselor.

STATEMENT IN REPLY TO SELECTIVE
SERVICE FORM 150

By: *David Wessel*

1. Describe the beliefs which are the basis for your claim
for classification as a conscientious objector.

> On the thirteenth of March, 1972, I registered, as
> required by law, with Local Board No. 9 (New Haven)
> of the Selective Service System. I did so after a great
> deal of reading, discussion, and thought. When I reg-
> istered, I presented a statement which said:

Today I reluctantly register with the Selective Service
System as required by law. I put the Selective Service
and the government of the United States on notice that
I shall struggle against the continued war in Indochina
with its massive aerial bombing and sophisticated electronic and automated battlefield.

This registration is not the end of my protest against
the policies of our government; it is not a surrender.
Rather it marks a new beginning, a new determination
to truly stop the killing, end the war, bring all my
brothers home, and see peace come to Indochina.

Today I take another step as I reply to the Selective
Service System's Special Form for Conscientious Objector (SSS Form 150, as revised April 18, 1972). I
cannot and will not serve in any capacity under the
Armed Forces of the United States nor will I engage
in so-called "alternate service" under the Selective Service System. The route to this decision is a lengthy one

which reflects years of thought; it will be part of me long past this day.

3. Explain how you acquired the beliefs which are the basis of your claim.

To determine how my beliefs were acquired is an impossible task. In 1968, I joined the Fellowship of Reconciliation and the Jewish Peace Fellowship, a step that was instrumental in my development as a conscientious objector. "The Fellowship of Reconciliation is composed of men and women who recognize the essential unity of mankind and have joined together to explore the power of love and truth for resolving human conflict."

As I prepared to make a decision on registration, I read *In Solitary Witness: The Life and Death of Franz Jagerstatter* by Gordon C. Zahn. The book describes the actions of an Austrian patriot who was beheaded by Hitler's forces for refusing to participate in the Nazi army even as a noncombatant. I am not a Franz Jagerstatter; I am not motivated by the same Christian fervor. Yet the book, which includes some of Jagerstatter's writings, begins to clarify the motivation behind one brave and very lonely martyr.

In a letter written to a young Hessian in 1899 by Leo Tolstoy (reprinted in Atlantic, February, 1968), Tolstoy argues that "*all just people must refuse to become soldiers.*" He simply and harshly defines a soldier as one "ready on another's command to kill all those ordered to kill." Slick public relations and intricate political argument cannot change the truth of Tolstoy's definition. I cannot agree totally with Tolstoy's statement that "Moral acts are distinguished from all other acts by the fact that they operate independently of any predictable advantage to ourselves or to others." But one analogy he uses is very appropriate and convincing. "If I find myself in a crowd of running people running with the crowd without knowing where, it is obvious that I have given myself up to mass hysteria; but if by chance I should push my way to the front, or be gifted with sharper sight than the others, or receive information that this crowd was racing to attack human beings and toward its own corruption, would I really not stop and tell the people what might rescue them? Would I go on running and do these things which I knew to be bad and corrupt? This is the situation of every individual called up for military service, if he knows what military service means."

Dan Berrigan has a short essay, "Meditation from Catonsville," in a book called *Delivered into Resistance* which was printed here in New Haven. In an often-repeated phrase, Berrigan says, "We have chosen to say, with the gift of our liberty, if necessary our lives: the violence stops here, the death stops here, the suppression of the truth stops here, this war stops here." And further in that same piece, "In a time of death, some men — the resisters, those who work hardily for social change, those who preach and embrace the unpalatable truth — such men overcome death, their lives are bathed in the light of resurrection, the truth has set them free. In the jaws of contumely, of good and ill report, they proclaim their love of their brethren." I too feel that I am part of that community of young men who had the guts to say NO to war and killing.

STATEMENT IN REPLY TO SELECTIVE SERVICE FORM 150

By: *Rees Rucker Shearer*

1. Describe the beliefs which are the basis for your claim for classification as a conscientious objector.

Destruction of human life is wrong. Murder as an end in itself is dealt with by criminal sanctions by this and other countries. Murder as a means of maintaining boundaries, power and "interests" is not only sanctioned by most governments — it is these governments themselves which perpetuate it.

There is, in my opinion, little justification for any kind of murder — even capital punishment, which is within the law and is overseen by a jury of the people. There is, in my opinion, *no* justification of the kind of murder exemplified by war. War indiscriminately kills and maims civilians and warriors alike; "warriors" who quite often do not know or comprehend the "cause" for which they are fighting. Many fight under duress and attempt to kill the young man on the other side who also, perhaps, is fighting under duress. These soldiers on opposing sides have never spoken to one another, yet they are forced into the moral predicament of holding power over each other's lives. Their only direction comes from anonymous orders. Officers tell them that the only answer is to "kill or be killed."

The cause I hear most often quoted these days is an insane paradox: "We are waging war in the interests of peace." That kind of 1984 "doublethink'" has duped millions to their death.[2]

War warps the minds of all who participate in it. The murder of one frightened peasant is the beginning of another massacre. Thousands of young men go into the army a little bit unsure of what they are doing. They are quickly swept up in the fateful course of events and *develop* some justification for the murders which they are ordered to perform. A little hardness must develop next, if they are to retain sanity — a hardeness which is difficult to dissolve once (and *if*) they make it home. And there are those whose minds *cannot* deal with the horrors they are ordered to commit and whose only recourse is withdrawal and creeping insanity.

But of what significance is the destruction of one man's life when now several nations have the power to destroy the entire natural world? For me, the murder, the destruction of one single person is the destruction of a whole world. Each man is important — the person is a part of the whole world and he is a microcosm of the order of things. In the words of John Donne:

Any man's death diminishes me, because I am involved in Mankind. And therefore never send to know for whom the bell tolls: it tolls for thee.
(Meditations XVIII 1624)

I also came to know and deeply respect the teachings of Christ. His words in the Sermon on the Mount are words of reconciliation and love, not hate and violence. You have heard that it was said, "An eye for an eye and a tooth for a tooth." But I say to you, Do not resist one who is evil. But if anyone strikes you on the

---

2. 1984 is the title of a book by George Orwell in which the Government, personified as "Big Brother," controls the minds and actions of people by means of an unlogical logic termed doublethink.

right cheek, turn to him the other also. . . . You have heard that it was said, "You shall love your neighbor and hate your enemy." But I say to you, Love your enemies and pray for those who persecute you, so that you may be sons of your Father who is in heaven.

(Matt. 5:38-41, 43-45)

Again, when Christ was captured in Gethsemane and one of his disciples retaliated against the captors, Christ rebuked him.
Then Jesus said to him, "Put your sword back into its place; for all who take the sword will perish by the sword."

(Matt. 26:52)

In both of these instances, Christ expresses the need to overcome evil with good, to respond with love rather than react with violence — even when your life is at stake. Admittedly this is a hard example to follow, but the imitation of Christ's actions is the duty of Christians. Christ showed us that there was another way — a loving way — to bring about change.

3. .Explain how you acquired the beliefs which are the basis of your claim.

I was raised in the absolute belief that murder in any form is wrong. I remember that my mother has always had grave doubts about the use of atomic bombs on the Japanese. My father has often spoken against capital punishment. They gave me the best education they knew how to give, always emphasizing the creative rather than the destructive, life rather than death. They taught me never to start a fight and to try to reason with someone whose views were in opposition to mine. Through childhood and young adulthood I attended church and Sunday School at the First Baptist Church of Clarendon in Arlington. Sometimes the Sunday school teachers found it hard to believe that I took the commandment "Thou shalt not kill" literally. But they never could show me acceptable qualifications on the commandment, and granted me my opinion.

Through junior high school and high school I often found myself in the position of mediator in the arguments between my friends. They talked of how their father served in World War II but I was proud that my father had found another way to serve his country and that as far back as the Civil War all of my ancestors had found civilian capacities in which to serve the United States. Ours was not a family of war stories. My grandmother, even though she was steeped in Virginia tradition, spoke harshly of the Civil War, its uselessness and its hardships.

STATEMENT IN REPLY TO SELECTIVE
SERVICE FORM 150

By: *Vincent Joseph Sweeney*

1. Describe the beliefs which are the basis for your claim
   for classification as a conscientious objector.

   > "Blessed are the peacemakers, for they shall be called
   > children of God."
   >
   > Matthew 5:9

   > "All who take the sword, will perish by the sword."
   > Matthew 26:52

   > "Enduring peace will come about not by countries
   > threatening each other but only through an honest
   > effort to create mutual trust."
   >
   > Albert Einstein

   > "Peace is not merely an end to war."
   > William Penn

   > "There is no hiding the fact that it is much harder to
   > be a Christian today than it was in the first centuries
   > and there is every reason to predict that it will be even
   > more difficult in the near future. When it becomes the
   > sacred duty of a man to commit sin, the Christian no
   > longer knows how he should live. There remains nothing
   > else for him to do but bear individual witness. And
   > where such witness, is, there is the Kingdom of God."
   >
   > Reinhold Scheider
   > (German poet and scholar)

It is time for me to bear individual witness. I can no longer serve Christ and the military at the same time.

3. Explain how you acquired the beliefs which are the basis of your claim.

Upon graduation from high school in 1969, I was advised by friends and relatives to join the Air National Guard. At that time, the ANG seemed a very logical enterprise. I did not want to be sent to war, simply for fear of dying, and it was almost a sure bet that I would not be sent there as a member of the ANG. I was counseled that this indeed was a fine way to fulfill my military obligation and felt no moral problems upon entering. But during basic training, I began to question many of the military's ways. When I went to the firing range at camp, I was surprised at the fact that we shot, not at bull's eye targets, but at silhouetted figures of man. We were instructed that the best place to hit the figure was in the heart, so he would not have a chance to live. For the first time, I started to question the morality of war. We were being trained to kill other human beings. I began to ask questions. And for answers, I started to look at the readings of Christ and took a second look at the religious training I had received all my life. I began to read the Bible more often than ever before. Christ was an amazing example to follow and the military was not following that life. I was not acting as I believed because I supported the military and its use of violence.
Since that spring of 1970, I kept searching for the best way to live. "Had non-violence only seemed convenient at the time?" Was I supporting war by being in the ANG? Was this mental depression I had experienced at guard drills related to my beliefs? Questions such as these do not come easily to answer. Filing for a Con-

scientious Objector claim is a very important step in one's life. I reflected on the situations, so as not to make any rash judgments, and in the fall of 1970, I decided that I was now a conscientious objector. My beliefs were now strong and permanent, and I then began to work on this paper.

When I began questioning myself and my role in the military, I also began to question my role in the Catholic Church. I began to examine the dogma and beliefs I had accepted all my life. I did not reject any of them, but only admitted that I was unsure of some of the beliefs. As I continued doing this, I became more religious than ever before. I saw how vital the Church was. The beliefs I now accepted were beliefs that my contemplation had verified, and not beliefs that I was given and never really saw what they meant. The Church and the good that it is striving for have become more important to me because of this period of questions and answers.

With this drastic period of change and turmoil going on inside myself, I often looked not only to my brother, but to my entire family. We have many diverse personalities in our family, and our problems are always overcome by the love we have for one another. Many times I looked at my father as an example. He was a man who was happy with life because he followed Christ's life as he believed he should. I am also trying to follow Christ's life in rejecting war and violence.
After rehashing the training I had received in my life and seeing if I could both serve the Church and the military, I found that I had no choice but to file for this claim. I saw problems in the local community, state and country, and then myself supporting the military war policy. So much manpower was being exerted on war policy and little was being done to constructively

help our brothers and sisters who had problems just living decently. I concluded that the ANG was in direct conflict with the training and beliefs I had received and lived throughout my life.

4. Explain what most clearly shows that your beliefs are deeply held.

Perhaps one of the most significant aspects of my life that exemplifies my beliefs is the fact that I have never physically struck another human being with the intent to harm them. In my nineteen years of living, I have never been in a fight.

I have never gone hunting in my life because of an abhorrence to killing anything, and the only time I have ever had a gun in my hands was at boot camp and at the ANG firing range. At both places, I received derogatory remarks because I did not know how to handle the weapon. Not being able to handle a gun is a direct result of my revulsion against any instrument that may be detrimental to mankind.

Finally, I have thought about this action for a long time. If the claim is approved, I would most likely have to stop going to school and move from Madison, my home for 19 years. I would be forced to move to a new environment with new people and new surroundings. This is something which would be very hard but I feel that it is worth the hard times it may temporarily cause. By leaving school, I would most likely lose any chance of playing baseball for the University of Wisconsin, a lifelong goal, not to mention the interruption of my progress toward a degree from the school. A CO is often looked down on by many people. I do not want people to dislike me for any reason, but the claim is something I feel Christ would have done.

STATEMENT IN REPLY TO SELECTIVE SERVICE FORM 150

By: *An Anonymous Objector*

1. Describe the nature of the beliefs which are the basis for your claim for classification as a conscientious objector.

> Rabbi Asher Block has written: "The Jews are a people who for well nigh two thousand years — with the single exception of Bar Kochba's second century revolt against Rome — never waged war." I can remember learning this in Hebrew School, and I am dismayed that a second exception has occurred within my lifetime, in fact just during the past year.
>
> The most basic teachings of the Jewish faith for me are first the well known "golden" rule, here as stated by Hillel:
>
> "What you would not have others do unto you, do not do unto others. . . . Love peace and pursue peace, love your fellow beings."
>
> I feel that I have always guided my actions by that rule, and it is most important for me to continue to do so. The second teaching that is most relevant here is the commandment: "Thou shalt not kill." (Exodus XX 13)
>
> The Jews do not celebrate any time in their history when they shed blood. David, who is one of the greatest of Jewish heroes, was a warrior, yet I was taught that we do not revere him for his military feats, but for his human qualities. The Lord refused to allow David his greatest wish, to build the great Temple, because he

had shed blood. Even when the Jews fled from captivity in Egypt and the Egyptians were drowning in the Red Sea, some angels rejoiced and were reprimanded as the Lord said, "How dare you sing, while the works of my hands are drowning?" The value of human life, even an enemy's, has always been a central concern of the Jews. Not only is it necessary for Jews to want peace and to pray for it, but we should "seek peace and pursue it." (Psalm 34:15). "The Law does not command you to run after or pursue the other commandments, but only to fulfill them upon the appropriate occasion. But peace you must seek in your own place and pursue it even to another place as well." This makes peace seeking, (and to me that means nonviolence as well) among the highest activities of man. "The commandment against killing corresponds to the commandment that we believe in God, for man is created in the divine image." I cannot overemphasize my feeling that the shedding of human blood is the worst of all offenses against both God and man, and I cannot commit such a transgression. Maimonides tells us: "Neither idolatry nor sexual immorality nor desecration of the sabbath is equal to bloodshed." For those are transgressions between man and God, while bloodshed is a crime between man and his fellow man. If one has committed this crime, he is deemed wholly wicked and all the good deeds he has performed during his lifetime cannot outweigh this crime or save him from judgment, as it is said, "A man that is laden with blood of any person shall hasten his steps to the pit; none will support him."

My Rabbi tells me that "The shedding of blood is regarded to be the worst criminal act possible, not only because it deprives another human being of his right to live, but also because it is the most serious form of sacrilege. Since man is created in the divine image, he who sheds blood diminishes the image of God within man." It is also commanded among the Jews that "with very few exceptions, every commandment of Judaism could be — and had to be — broken whenever human life was at stake."

I view my belief in the Supreme Being as outlined above, and the sanctity of human life as prescribed by that being, if I am to follow my belief religiously, I cannot shed the blood of another man.

Another distinction that deserves clarification is that between force and violence. It has been taught if one was pursuing his fellow man to slay him, and the pursued could have saved himself by maiming a limb of the pursuer, but instead killed his pursuer, the pursued is subject to punishment on that account.

I could not kill, even in self-defense. "In every other law of the Torah, if a man is commanded 'Transgress and suffer not death,' he may transgress and not suffer death, excepting idolatry, incest, and shedding blood. . . . Murder may not be practiced to save one's life." (Sanhedrin, 74a) War is violence, and I could not participate in such an action.

3. Explain how you acquired the beliefs which are the basis of your claim.

In Religious School from ages 9-13, where I was an honor student, and while attending religious services at the Temple, I became acquainted with the basic teachings of the Jewish Religion. I was especially affected by the importance attached to human life and the elaborate laws dealing with the treatment of Human Beings. The Torah and the Talmud are the basic scriptures for Jewish training and living, and of the Torah it is said, "All her paths are peace!" This is even more true of the Talmud.

The works of Gandhi, Martin Luther King, Jr., and Martin Buber, the late Jewish theologian, have influenced me. Friends and relatives, most of whom don't agree with me, have challenged me to consider deeply the implications of my convictions, and I now know myself sufficiently to refuse to be placed into a position where action is demanded of me which I cannot reconcile with a lifetime of conviction.

STATEMENT IN REPLY TO SELECTIVE SERVICE FORM 150

By: *An Anonymous Objector*

1. Describe the beliefs which are the basis for your claim for classification as a conscientious objector.

It is my belief that only individual human lives are sacred. All material goods are secondary to the needs of man for life and his freedom to act as a moral being. The distinctly human, and hence highest, character of man is his ability to reflect on questions of right and wrong independent of material self-interest. Man without such moral autonomy is but an atom-smashing animal.

Man's ability to act in a selfless way, for the good of all humanity, is the basis of the belief in man's status as being made in the image of God. The Bible tells us that man has such semi-divine status by virtue of the very Act of Creation. Man has the potential to act in accordance with God's will (i.e., man has the potential to act as a morally autonomous being). The cornerstone of such Godliness is the respect for all men as autonomous beings. Men may not be treated as things, for other ends. The only moral end is man himself, morally autonomous man. To treat another man as a means is to deny the humanity of both the actor and the "object." To treat oneself as a means to some other end is similarly to degrade oneself to non-divine status, to relegate one's humanity to a secondary position.

The question of war must be seen in the same framework that all moral questions must be put in: What will the effect of such action be upon the humanity (i.e., Godliness) of those whom I confront? What will be the effect of my action upon my own moral autonomy? In such a decision, all those involved must be considered as individual moral beings, made of the same stuff as all of us are. Each person has the potential for Godliness, for moral autonomy, and must always be seen in such a light. According to various genetic and environmental factors, an individual may or may not attain such status. However, our own actions can become a factor in the environmental nurturing of the expression of humanity in others. This factor is key to all moral decisions.

Given my religious outlook, I find the military to be an immoral institution for a number of reasons. On the most obvious level, the military is founded on the negation of individual moral autonomy. Not only must the soldier regard other people as things, he must himself be regarded as a thing. The military destroys human morality in all that it touches. The soldier must cede his very right to make moral decisions. Decisions to kill, burn, torture, etc., are made *despite* moral considerations. The soldier kills because he is told to do so. He burns down a village because those are his orders. He murders prisoners because they represent a hindrance to the larger strategy, formulated by some unknown other. Men who might otherwise enjoy each other's company are reduced to the bestiality of determining the worth of the other's life by the color of his uniform.

The second, and perhaps less obvious, aspect of my opposition to the military is its general effect, its impact on the greater human community. This broad question involves such questions as why wars are fought and what they accomplish. The history of human warfare indicates that all warring nations have believed their side to be right, their cause to be just. Rarely has a nation stated its intentions in making war in any but moral terms. This nation has used such terms as "manifest destiny," "the war to end all wars," and "war to bring freedom to those threatened by Communist aggression." The United States has not been alone, however, in using moralistic slogans to rationalize greed and a lust for power. The Nazis had their divine mission. The Russians had their campaign to keep the world safe for socialism. The British have sought to Christianize the African savages. In short, each nation finds little difficulty in rationalizing their warmaking in moral terms. Most people, mesmerized by their nationalism, never question the merit of their cause.

As long as men continue to justify warmaking in moral terms, they will continue to make war. No nation powerful enough to defeat another will go for long before discovering some moral grounds for conquering the other. The only way that war will end is by the renunciation of any grounds for making war. Everyone now agrees that no nation should go to war in order to augment its own wealth, and, as a result, no nation now states its war goals in such terms. If all men similarly refused to accept a moralistic justification for war, wars would not be fought. The only way to end war, then, is for all men to refuse to countenance the waging of war. Such a decision can only be made by the morally autonomous individual. The individual must renounce military means for solving problems.

For both these religious and practical reasons I am opposed to participation in the military. I will not support the efforts of the military in any way. I will not kill, nor contribute to killing, on the basis of uniform coloration. I cannot cede my stature as a morally autonomous being (made in the image of God) to a "higher in command." I must make my own moral decisions at all times. I firmly believe that "moral" justifications of war are fully as dangerous as material justifications, and I thus will not be a party to either. If drafted, I will refuse to serve in the military.

2. Will your beliefs permit you to serve in a position in the armed forces where the use of weapons is not required? If not, why?

As I have written previously, I feel that the only way that man will bring an end to the horrors of war is for each individual to refuse to support war efforts. The soldiers who do not do the actual killing are as responsible as those who pull the trigger for the waging of war. Without supply officers and medics, there would be no military. It would be a great victory for peace if all doctors and medics refused to serve in the military. This action would be in the best interest of the health of all those who in the future might otherwise require medical aid.

I have no objection to ministering to the sick and injured civilian population.

3. Explain how you acquired the beliefs which are the basis of your claim.

In the past three years, I have wavered between applying and not applying for CO status. I spoke with my father, with other rabbis and ministers, and with friends about this decision. I meanwhile read extensively in pacifist literature, from Gandhi's autobiography to Einstein's essays on peace. I did not apply for CO status when I was 18 years old for two reasons. Firstly, I felt that I would have enlisted and fought in World War II, and that this sentiment would invalidate any CO claim. Secondly, I felt that the draft system was as unconscionable as war itself, and that I could not in good conscience cooperate with it.

I have only recently resolved these two problems fully in my own mind. I do not see any wars such as World War II recurring. The wars of the present and the future that the United States will be involved in will be wars that will produce only hatred and misery. Even wars of national defense, such as the Israeli case, lead only to heightened hatred without resolving any basic problems. The only way to bring about peace in the atomic age, indeed the only way to preserve humanity, is to unilaterally renounce war as an instrument of national policy.

STATEMENT IN REPLY TO SELECTIVE
SERVICE FORM 150

By: *An Anonymous Objector*

1. Describe the beliefs which are the basis for your claim
    for classification as a conscientious objector.

> My commitment not to participate in war stems from
> my beliefs in the supreme value of human life. This
> conviction is founded on a belief in God, though it is
> a God different from the one traditionally accepted. The
> God I speak of is not something spiritually or meta-
> physically "up there" or "out there," but is rooted in all
> human souls. God is the depth and ground of all being;
> depth, not height, is what the word God means. To
> comprehend this use of the term God, you must "think
> of the depths of your life, of the source of your being,
> of your ultimate concern, of what you take seriously
> without reservation" (Paul Tillich). The word God does
> not denote a Being, but rather the meaning of our exist-
> ence, what for one is ultimate reality.
> To kill, no matter how "worthy" or "noble" the cause,
> is to destroy a spirit that is intrinsically sacred, to
> destroy the God that is the ultimate ground of every-
> one's life. It its wrong and thus I cannot participate
> in war.

3. Explain how you acquired the beliefs which are the basis
    of your claim.

> It is difficult to detail experiences that led to the for-

171

mation of my ideas but certainly one is being witness to the realities of war and death. When confronted with the actuality of death, I began to realize the great beauty of life and also to realize that persons are more imporant than standards. Many of my attitudes were stimulated by the writings of Hermann Hesse, Paul Tillich, and A. J. Muste, among others. Perhaps the book that finalized my religious views was *Honest to God* by John A. T. Robinson. Many of my beliefs, and thus much of what I said in response to the first question, were first impressed upon me by this work. Also, last summer, and continuing onward, I was involved in relationships with a few people which illustrated to me that what I felt to be the real nature of man and God was true, and this strongly buttressed my convictions. I am unable to isolate further incidents but can only say that it was a total awakening brought about by the factors mentioned above and others. Implicit in my conception of religion is the idea that it is not possible to separate faith from action or belief from occupation.

5. Have you ever given expression publicly or privately, written or oral, to the views herein expressed as the basis of your claim? Give examples.

I have participated in numerous demonstrations protesting the war in Vietnam, the most recent of which were: the October 15 moratorium, the November 14 and 15 march against death, and the activities held Christmas Eve in New York's Central Park. Not only have I marched, but have been active on the Moratorium Committee and I have canvassed and leafleted numerous neighborhoods. Last month I attended the Central Park memorial rally in memory of Martin Luther King, Jr., and I intend to continue to be active in such activities.

STATEMENT IN REPLY TO SELECTIVE SERVICE FORM 150

By: *An Anonymous Objector*

1. Describe the beliefs which are the basis for your claim for classification as a conscientious objector.

> I believe in a Supreme Being, which I have learned to refer to as God, but to which all cultures have turned their highest sentiments under many names. He is the creator of life. I see the preservation and respect for life as the principal responsibility of man toward his God. While I realize that accident and human passions often account for the destruction of life in this imperfect world, I believe that organizing society in military fashion for social ends, with the express method of killing as a means to even the highest social ends, is both a violation of man's obligation to God as creator and an immoral blasphemous act of defiance.
> There is much in basic Jewish doctrine to substantiate this belief. But one need go no further than the most basic of Jewish law, the Ten Commandments. These are God's words to man governing man's actions in society. Several of the commandments are particularly relevant to my conscientious objection to any form of military service. At the center, of course, is the first commandment, which makes very clear the supreme and unique relationship between God and man. The second commandment demands that we have no other God before us, nor worship any other graven image.

In many ways the modern nation is the Golden Calf of our own times. I do not feel alienated from American society; on the contrary, I hope to play a full role in the field of education, one of the most important areas of contribution to the community. But I do feel I must draw the distinction between complete engagement in society and its rightful pursuits, and the substitution of the state for God as the source of some moral imperative to take life. If some intellectual historians are correct in assessing nationalism as the religion of modern times and the nation-state as God, let me dissent. I am an atheist in the face of this modern faith, and deny that any loyalty but to God can demand complete submission. I believe in the God of the Bible who created all humans as humans, and not as Americans, Germans, Russians and Chinese. I believe that the nation cannot demand a life which it does not give. In relation to the third commandment, I believe that using God's name in the service of violations of the commandments of God is quite the quintessence of taking the Lord's name in vain. That very practice, however, is the explicit and implicit claim of all armies — now and in the past. They would kill although God commands "Thou shalt not kill," and then claim that very action to be a Godly one.

As for the Fifth Commandment, the statement is simple: "Thou shalt not murder." There is no qualification, no dispensation, no excuse. Murder is murder, and murder by any other name is still the job of the military organization of any nation, including the United States. I cannot allow myself to become any part of that organization or any organization which kills and orders one to kill. Crimes of passion and killing in direct self-defense are still sins before God, but perhaps are partially understandable under certain circumstances. But the malicious, premeditated military system of killing for social and political objectives is nothing more or less than one of the worst crimes of defiance against God and humanity. I refuse to have any part in such a process.

I might say a word about my concept of guilt in terms of a war. First of all, I think the greatest guilt in war must be laid to those who participate in war while knowing better morally. I include myself among those who know, and I cannot turn back on this position if I am to live with myself for the rest of my life. As for those who prosecute war for ideological or political reasons, I find Hannah Arendt's explanation of the Nazi phenomenon quite convincing. Evil is simply banal. People who cannot or do not care to tell the difference between right and wrong roads to personal or societal goals are too limited in their humanity to realize that killing humans cannot possibly help humanity. In my view there are great political and social causes, for which I have and would make great sacrifice, short of death and its concomitant of killing. But no social goal can ever be held to be more important than God-given life. Others may disagree, and I would condemn them in so far as they took the lives of others into their plans. Military service is the extreme version of that which I would condemn. It forces people to kill people and be killed for the "false God of the state." It incidentally implies that those who survive should modify their belief in the real God to make room for worship of the state. I cannot abide such a practice.

AMENDED STATEMENT IN REPLY TO SELECTIVE SERVICE FORM 150

Communicated in a personal letter
by Bob Miller

The format that I used to convince my draft board of my sincerity was artificial in ways because I played their games. I used the right terminology and was careful of the traps they set. Thus, the essence of my beliefs were sometimes watered-down in the written form.

However, I claimed then, and claim still, that by reason of my religious training and belief, I am conscientiously opposed to participation in *war* of any form, past, present or future. I present my case very simply and honestly. My religious training and beliefs consist simply of following the words and actions of Jesus Christ, and therefore under the circumstances could I justify killing another person or support those who could justify any form of war?

The teachings of Jesus Christ aren't the most logical or rational ideas for mankind, but you must admit that they are the most humane. For example, who is going to love their enemies and pray for those who mistreat them? (Matt. 5:43-44) Those who listen to and live Christ's words of unlimited love will respond. Those with retaliation or even limited love will not. What is the effectiveness of non-retaliation, you might say. Well, "many Christians are willing to back up their belief in this idea with their lives, which within itself is a strong argument."[3] The argument of practicality is irrelevant: I am bound by higher loyalty other than my country. My interpretation of Scripture and the acts of Jesus are not at all original thoughts. Most of my beliefs have been brought into focus by the early Christians, and men such as Clarence Jordan, Dan and Phil Berrigan, Martin Luther King, and all the people that dare to *live* the Gospel.

------

3. Clarence Jordan, "Sermon on the Mount."

AMENDED STATEMENT IN REPLY TO SELECTIVE SERVICE FORM 150

By: *An Anonymous Objector*

My application for conscientious objector status is based on the belief that killing, be it in the form of war, capital punishment or whatever, is morally wrong. I cannot under any circumstances condone the taking of the life of another human being.

I am a Roman Catholic and thus a Christian. The basic premise and rule of Christianity is to "love God and your fellow man." I believe that all men are my brothers and that I am commanded to love all men. Thus my beliefs go beyond the rejecting of war to the rejecting of all forms of killing. Clearly, however, it does include war as a moral wrong which I must not participate in.

As a member of the Roman Catholic Church, I do have some guidelines for objecting to war. The Church has stated four rules for a "justifiable war" which in essence condemn all wars which have been fought and recorded in history. The Church says that a war must be a defensive war in which civilians are not involved and no unnecessary destruction of life or property occurs and that restitution must be made for all damage done. In my opinion, if these four conditions were met, a war could not occur.

I believe that one's life is a sacred thing and that it is something which no one has the right to take except God. I believe that no one may take the life of another human being for any reason, and that to do so is a moral wrong.

In summary, the nature of my belief is that no one has the right to take the life of another human being and this belief is based upon my belief in God and the sanctity of life.

I suppose it would be fair to say that my beliefs have been developing over the last 22 years. I was born of Roman Catholic parents and educated in Catholic schools. I was taught and believed that to kill another human being is against the law of God. Issues such as war were never fully discussed and I was led to believe that it might be a necessary evil.

When I graduated from high school and went to college, I left behind the people who always told me what was right and what was wrong, and for the first time I was forced to think things out and decide for myself. My college years have resulted in the changing of many attitudes, some more than others. However, looking back I can see how the beliefs I now hold about killing developed. There were many influences: courses I took, friends, participation in activities and most importantly participation in religious activities at Church. I became involved with a movement called Antioch. I became a member of a team which conducted weekend retreats and discussions for students. These weekends consisted of talks by students on fundamental principles of Christianity and their application to the lives of students. As I worked on talks such as "The Life of a Christian" I began to realize that there really is one basic commandment and that is "to love God and all men." I have two close friends and after many long discussions with them, I came to the realization that killing is morally wrong and that I cannot condone it under any circumstances.

To try to list everything that has influenced me in reaching this belief would be impossible, but undoubtedly my association with the people on these weekends and my participation in them were the most profound influences. I first became involved with the Antioch movement about three and one-half years ago. I did not develop my beliefs instantly but through giving talks on the weekends, reading many books (religious and philosophical) and long discussions with friends and priests these beliefs have developed.

178

I do not think that these beliefs are a "passing thing" because I have considered them for some time now and they continue to grow stronger. A fair question would be, "Why have you waited until now to declare that you are a CO?" I guess there are several reasons. First of all, *I am a typical person* and I usually put things off when they don't seem to be of a pressing nature. As long as I had a II-2 classification I really didn't worry about it and always put off making a final decision. When I received my I-A, however, I was forced to sit down and think everything through and to make a final decision. It was not until then that I realized that there was cause for hurry in applying for conscientious objector status. It took about two weeks to finally reach a decision on what type of CO I should request. I finally decided on 1-0 for the reasons given in the following question.

My beliefs do not restrict me from ministering to the sick and injured. They do, however, restrict me to doing so outside of the military. The purpose of all men in military service is to insure military victory. The Army Field Manual FM 8-10, page 195, states: "The primary duty of medical troops as of all other troops is to contribute their utmost to the success of the command of which the medical service is a part." I do not believe in killing and therefore cannot condone the act even if performed by someone else. If I were to serve as a non-combatant in the army, I would be serving to help insure a military victory which would be gained through killing. This, to me, would mean that I would be condoning the action taken to attain that victory which would include the taking of the lives of others. Therefore, I cannot accept serving as a non-combatant.

I can, however, minister to the sick and injured outside of the military because to do so would not be to insure a military victory, but to help my brother. This would include caring for wounded soldiers who are out of the service. These men do not have an effect upon the army and ministering to them would not be in opposition to my beliefs.

LETTER BY AN ANONYMOUS OBJECTOR
TO HIS FRIENDS

Dear Friends,

All of us, uninclined though we are to take unpopular or dangerous stands, occasionally reach points of decision where we must either stand up for something or die a little bit inside by failing to do so, and become a little bit less of a person. I have reached such a point, and I need the help and support of all those people, whether they agree with my decision or not, who know me as a person of integrity and trust the sincerity of my convictions.

I have written today to my draft board, and shared with them my conviction that I cannot in good conscience participate in war. Many of you know some of the uncertainties I have been through on this question: trying to decide whether I should

(1) simply wait out the decision and accept induction with the reasonable expectation that my poor eyesight would keep me out of actual combat,

(2) go to Air Force Officer Candidate School with the reasonable expectation of noncombatant desk work and perhaps learning something, or

(3) take the risky and at times unnecessary decision of applying for conscientious objector status, which would of course have eliminated the second option, as well as being a step of such magnitude that I have not until now been sure my belief is deep enough to stake my career and life on it.

I have shared my uncertainties on the first two options

with my draft board in the past — in fact, as recently as last March I wrote to them reaffirming my belief in the present American policy of holding the line in Vietnam — and in spite of my explaining to them that I believe in holding that line by rendering assistance rather than violence, it is going to be understandably more difficult for me to convince them of the sincerity of a belief reached after spiritual turmoil, than it would be for someone who had been raised all his life in the theory and practice of absolute pacifism.

I have every reason to believe that the members of my draft board are also men of great sincerity and conscience, who carry the very difficult burden of having to judge the sincerity of others. They must ask and understand why I have only now become sure of my convictions; yet no man can prove his sincerity by what he says. I can tell them what the immediate reasons are for deciding now:

(1)   My realization just this summer, travelling home from the Peace Corps via East Europe, that the people of communist countries, even their soldiers are pretty average, real human beings rather than just abstract "enemies."

(2)   Seeing the incredibly brave and disciplined nonviolent resistance of the Czechs (many of whom I had met just a few weeks before). The effect of their nonviolent protest on the Russian army and on the world was a force for good, far greater than any amount of violence could have been, and, finally.

(3)   As I return to America after two years abroad and take up my role as an adult American, I realize that the time has come for me to act on what I have learned, and on what I believe in. I am at the pivotal point where I have the perspective and the obligation to set my future in the light of my past.

I have not come to conscientious objection by sudden "conversion." I have been procrastinating for a long time. The sincerity of my beliefs can be attested only by the people who have known me and have followed my life as it wound its way up to that decision.

The issue for me is not Vietnam, nor is it my loyalty to my country. The *issue is war itself,* and whether my conscience and religious beliefs allow me to take part in it in pursuit of *any end.* My answer is NO. In concrete terms, war demands:

(1) that I give my highest allegiance to my country, even at the expense of my religious values and my human concern.

(2) that I kill (or directly assist and support others who are killing) other men in the name of a goal which my country's leaders consider more important than the lives expended in achieving these goals, and

(3) that I either accept killing or destruction into my value system, or deny that I am individually responsible and accountable for my actions.

Stated that way, I think most people would agree that war is the diametric opposite of Christian teaching. Christianity is the "gospel of Love," whose primary tenets are (1) to love and serve God above all else (including one's nation), and (2) to love your fellow man as thyself. Christianity proclaims *love;* in fact, it commands us to love even in the face of violence.

Many sincere and articulate men argue that in an imperfect world such as ours, war is the lesser of a variety of existing evils, and that therefore, we must learn to swallow our consciences, serve our time, and hope for the best. I cannot accept this for myself. To do so would mean renouncing my belief in responding to today's problems. That I cannot and will not affirm.

I have been asked whether it is not just as wrong or worse to stand by while innocent people are oppressed. To this I answer: Yes, but

(1) The weapons of modern warfare are just as likely to kill the victims of oppression as the oppressors

(2) To wish an end to oppression does not include meeting violence with more violence, and

(3) If I must choose between failing to do something which *might* be right, and actively doing something which I know quite certainly to be both wrong and sinful (mass killing), my decision must be to avoid what I know with certainty to be wrong, while at the same time giving all my energies to set right whatever wrongs I can, but do so in the Christian way, i.e., nonviolent manner.

I ask your help, not to support me nor even to agree with me, but to bear witness for me and the ideals I stand for.

Please address your letter to "The Chairman, Local Board No. . . ." My decision has been a long time in coming, but now my time has run out, as it has for all of us.

EXCERPTS FROM STATEMENTS IN REPLY
TO SELECTIVE SERVICE FORM 150

By: *An Anonymous Conscientious Objector*

To bear witness as a Jew to the spirit of God in my own life has been important to me since I was a child. I feel great social responsibility for my actions, for the Jewish tradition of the lamedvovnik teaches that the fate of the world may rest on the holy act of a handful of good men. My faith in God and in the possibility of miracles — an element of Jewish tradition in which I believe very strongly and which is a very important part of my religious faith, impels me to believe that acts of goodness and holiness, inspired by love, trust, and willing sacrifice and suffering, may have a redeeming power that can transform the world. And I feel that every commission of evil by one who knows an action to be wrong may likewise have an ultimate significance far greater than its author intended or wished. "It is a terrible thought, that an individual wrongdoing melts into the great mass of human crime, and makes us — who dreamed only of our own little separate sin — makes us guilty of the whole." This reflection by a character in Nathaniel Hawthorne's *The Marble Faun* (Chapter XIX) made a deep impression on me when I read it as a senior in high school. A single murder indeed makes one guilty of all the murders that have ever been committed, for whatever personal or national loyalty; as it is written in the Talmud, "Whosoever destroys a single soul, Scripture imputes guilt to him as though he had destroyed a whole world" (Sanhedrin 37a).

184

I have learned from my own experience, and through others as related in non-violence seminars, of the power of gentleness and understanding to disarm wrath, distrust and hostility, and to evoke respect, humaneness and an equal good will. And the historical record of non-violent protest and resistance movements (in Hungary, Finland, South Africa, and elsewhere) would seem to bear out Aldous Huxley's contention that "even when used sporadically and unsystematically (as has been the case up till now), the method of non-violence actually works and . . . can be used by quite ordinary people. . . ."[4] I feel that the practice of non-violence as a way of life, and the use of non-violent methods to resist evil institutions and change oppressive social systems, offer mankind's best hope for survival, and for the eventual establishment of a society based on brotherly love, free from oppression towards anyone.

STATEMENT IN REPLY TO SELECTIVE SERVICE FORM 150

By: *An Anonymous Objector*

1. Describe the nature of your belief which is the basis for your claim and state why you consider it to be based on religious training and belief.

A saying that has gained some circulation in contemporary society states, "Suppose they gave a war and nobody came?" The question is a Utopian one, to be sure, but one that bears directly on the reason that I am opposed to participation in war in any form and unable to take any part in it. Each man that participates is guilty of a crime. A song of the youth of our country says, "He's the Universal Soldier and he really is to blame. . . ." And he is. If every Universal Soldier refused to kill other men — men different from him only in the color of their uniforms, then those who rule would have to seek another way of settling their disputes. Admittedly, that day is a long way off, but that in no way excuses those who see the truth from obeying it. It is not enough to wait for everyone else to first come around, nor is it enough to wait to be the second man to act morally; one must be the first and await the others, though it may be a long and painful wait. To do otherwise would be to be doomed to moving continually backward, and never forward. Each man must do what his religion and his conscience dictate, and refuse to do what he sees as wrong and sinful. Even the military recognizes that an illegal order does not expiate the man guilty of carrying out a crime. I see participation in war as just such a situation.

My duty to my religion, myself and my fellow man dictates that I must say no to the directive to take part in war in any form. For some, that might be enough; for myself, it is not. I feel I must try not only to avoid being a negative force, but to be a positive one — to try to end all wars and to try to minimize the damage of those wars that do come to pass as best I can. My medical training lends itself to just such a task, and in this I am fortunate. To misuse this training would be a double negation of all in which I believe — a double "sin," if you will. It is something I would not do under any threat.

2. Explain how, when and from whom or from what source you received the religious training and acquired the religious belief which is the basis of your claim.

Early in high school I read the works of Immanuel Kant that had an effect on probably every decision I have made in subsequent years. I must say that much of what he wrote was far above my head. I have forgotten most of his exact words, but one quote has stuck with me almost intact. This sentence alone probably was the greatest factor in my development during those years. Immanuel Kant wrote. "Make each decision in your life such, if that if each man made all his decisions in that same way, the world would be a better place for all men." In some ways it is little more than the Golden Rule.

His dictum was to be the "working arm" of my religion. Here was a simple rule for most every situation, from cheating on exams to littering, to telling jokes about Negro kids. With it, I knew it would never be me who closed the gas chamber door, or pulled the trigger, or even withheld money from the poor.

Although I cannot point to any single incident that crystalized my opposition to the war, I decided quite early that it was a tragic error. No argument proffered in its defense could hold the slightest hope of outweighing the depth and scope of the misery that was being visited on the people of that tiny country, and on my own country as well. With this conviction, I began writing letters and picketing while still in high school. If there were any imperative for a religious man in the world, it seemed it would be to put an end to that horror. My efforts are still continuing in this direction.

APPLICATION FOR DISCHARGE ON GROUNDS OF CONSCIENTIOUS OBJECTION

By: *An Anonymous Former Soldier*

I strongly believe that war in any form is never in accordance with the will of God, and that no social institution does greater damage to human life and personality than does war. These beliefs are central not only to my worship during meetings, but also to my daily life. My religious testimony is a positive one in that it is an essential part of my beliefs to apply pacifism constructively to concrete situations in the service of mankind. Hence, alternative service is an essential ingredient of my religious faith and practice.

Furthermore, at this time I wish to renounce my military oath, for it is contradictory with my Quaker faith and practice. I regard the taking of an oath as contrary to the teaching of Christ, and as setting up a double standard of truthfulness, whereas sincerity and truth should be practiced in all the dealings of life (Cf. Quaker Message, p. 66).

"We utterly deny all outward wars and strife, and fightings with outward weapons, for any end, or under any pretense whatsoever; this is our testimony to the whole world. The Spirit of Christ, by which we are guided, is not changeable, so as once to command us from a thing as evil and again to move into it; and we certainly know and testify to the world, that the Spirit of Christ, which leads us into all truth, will never move us to fight and war against any man with outward weapons, neither for the Kingdom of Christ nor for

189

the kingdoms of the world. . . . Therefore, we cannot learn war any more."

—A Declaration from the Quakers presented to King Charles II, 1660.

III

One discovery that seems to emerge from the reading of the many diverse C.O. statements is that the one conviction shared by every objector is the strong intuition that war in general and modern war most decidedly violates specifically the 5th Commandment, "Thou shalt not kill." That injunction is believed to be absolute and irrevocable, and compliance with it supersedes the demand for obedience to any other authority, whether legally constituted or not.

No one, even after the most extensive search of the scriptures, could come up with any passage that cites war or any other common social enterprise as a qualifying clause amending the 5th Commandment, "Thou shalt not kill."

The question of whether to participate in war and engage in mass killing in pursuit of a national purpose has always posed an even more troublesome dilemma to a Jew than to a Christian. The Christian motto, "Give unto Caesar what belongs to Caesar," that guided the relationship between organized religion and body politic for so long in Europe, coupled with the American tradition of the separation of Church and State, provided an escape clause for churches that freed them of responsibility of intervening when, in the name of collective goals formulated by either Kings, Emperors or Fuehrers, nations came into conflict with the moral law. The Jewish religion, having never subscribed to the "Give unto Caesar what belongs to Caesar" motto, was never relieved from the responsibility of judging nations. The tradition of the prophets has been one of consistent and unrelenting haranguing of the Kings to return to the ways of righteousness and to conform to the precepts of the Torah.

190

To Jewish religious doctrine, being less metaphysical in outlook than Christianity, but intensely concerned with the pursuit of justice, the proposition that religion shall be the arbiter only of conduct of the private individual but must scrupulously refrain from judging the conduct of men when engaged in collective action, is totally unacceptable. There emerges for the Jew and Christian alike, who accepts as a binding document of moral authority either the Gospel or what is referred to as "The Old Testament," a moral dilemma that was made intensely acute by the war in Vietnam, but will surface again in future wars.

The question of what to do when a secular law or policy of a state violates the "command" of the Torah or Gospel is a tricky one for any religious person. It is obviously absurd to propose that every act of domestic or foreign policy be subjected first to clerical scrutiny before deciding whether faithful Jewish or Christian citizens can give their allegiance and obedience to them.

Who is going to decide whether a war is just or unjust? We have no reliable agencies that can rate wars for us and certify with authority on their morality. The conscientious objector rejected, however, government as the most unreliable agency to carry out such an estimate for us. Since, on the other hand, in agreement with a recent Supreme Court ruling, one cannot possibly reserve to any single individual the privilege of arbitrarily distinguishing when to agree to participate in war and when to refuse on grounds of conscience, the conscientious objector proposed that we adopt as a moral guideline the assumption that all wars are most probably evil. Those who returned from even the briefest excursion into theology came back with the certainty that the chance that all wars are sinful was so great, that participation in any of them should be avoided and refused. Many who listened to the religious arguments of the conscientious objectors suspected that they were faked. The skeptics probably rightly perceived that the pursuit of theology merely made most young people discover that the sentiments they felt were merely expressed more beautifully and in more majestic terms by the prophets than by the modern authors, who first instilled these thoughts in them during their secular education.

The existence of a GOD, and his relationship to Man was politely ignored. One of the reasons for the reluctance to come to terms with the idea of GOD, was that the concept of an all-powerful, all-merciful and all-just God, who seems to distribute his favors so unequally, turned out to be too big a theological stumbling block. To a generation that learned about the holocaust in school, and watched an updated mini-version repeat performance on television 365 days a year for almost seven years all the stock answers provided by organized religion to the haunting question, "Why are some spared when others must perish?", sounded contrived at best and blasphemous at worst.

If God is all-knowing, all-powerful, and all-good, how is it that He allows evil in the world? Conventional religious answers take these forms; "What you and I may think is evil is not really evil at all. It is just our faulty interpretation of what we see around us." Christian Science is the best illustration of this attitude. The malady does not really exist; it is only the product of man's sinful imagination and his succumbing to the inclination of that imagination. The second response would have us believe that in the mind of God what we see as evil is really an instrumentality of some ultimate good. There are many assurances that in another order of existence we will see what God had in mind. "In the divine order of nature both life and death, joy and sorrow, serve beneficent ends, and in the fullness of time we shall know why we are tried and why our love brings us sorrow as well as happiness." *I would not categorically deny this possibility, but its staunchest defenders would have to admit that the evidence for this position is very weak indeed.* If God were responsible for the evil in this world, He would not be fit for human worship. He would not deserve to be prayed to or thought about.*

All of these contradictions could fall into place like the missing part of a jig saw puzzle once we can bring ourselves to admit that God is *not* all powerful.

Those of us both young and old who tried to fit religious doctrines to our modern dilemma and anxieties were least impressed by the divine property of power, possibly because the concept of power arouses such suspicions and distrust.

The concept of a finite God is not a strange one — neither to theologists nor scientists. The original idea comes from Edgar Sheffield Brightman in his book "A Philosophy of Religion." "God may be omniscient, He may be omnipresent, but according to this view, He is not omnipotent; He is not all-powerful. This view of God puts forth the idea that there is something in this universe beyond the grasp, beyond the control and beyond the power of God. It is a kind of internal obstruction and a kind of irrationality over which God has no control. Technically this is known by the term 'the given.'"

In the finite theistic concepts of God, God needs us as much as we need Him, for man is the instrument of the fulfillment of God's incomplete creation. Generations may go by without any visible signs of progress, but there is progress. For me the theory of the finite God is the more coherent view that takes account of the factual situation of the world with all its evil and seeming irrationalities, and still permits a God that can be called good.*

A similar concept has been embraced by scientists based on aesthetic considerations.

The grandeurs of a God who sets into motion the drama of evolution would be greatly diminished should he insist on constant and repeated intervention and interference with the execution of the grand design.

----

*From a sermon delivered by Rabbi Gustav Buchdahl on The Finite God.

Every act of creation carries with it the loss of control, lest the product be robots rather than creatures.

These metaphysical considerations aside, the only thing that made sense was the Kennedy admonition that privilege carries with it obligation, and that the recipients of mercy inherit also awesome responsibilities.

It is, perhaps, presumptuous of the author to stray so far from his own field of competence and review theological arguments which, upon examination by better qualified and more learned authorities, may turn out to be indefensible. These thoughts are, however, presented not so much as finished conclusions to be accepted or rejected, but rather they are offered as a report of the reflection and the debates that, however erroneous and naive they may seem if measured by more scholarly standards, nevertheless propelled some men into action and influenced them to make choices that changed their own lives and in some small measure perhaps the lives of all of us.

EPILOGUE

As I am sending these pages to the publisher, the passions that stimulated them to be written, have subsided and the dangers that had aroused them seem to have receded. Other issues, some more compelling, some more direct and immediate, have competed for our attention and claimed our concern. But, for a brief moment during the terrible decade of the 60's, some of us, both young and old, were seized by a sense of revulsion. We revolted against our own cruelty, or lust, our greed — or vanity, our lack of compassion, our pride, but most of all against the inertia of our hearts. We put our minds, but most of all, our souls to work to find an escape route that would link us up with the road to the "Good Life."

Needless to say, we did not find the road. We did not escape but ran around in circles. What transpired during those few years on the campuses may have been nothing more than a ripple — perhaps no more significant than the Peasants' Revolt in 13th-century Germany or the Whiskey Rebellion in George Washington's United States.

I should like to think, however, that memories of events neither get lost nor are they ever quite forgotten by the minds that experience them.

Just like our generation once flirted with far out — sometimes with radical — schemes, and then formed the solid majority that voted in New Deal Reforms, Welfare State and Socialized Medicine, so perhaps the minds of the Flower Children and of the War Protesters and the Draft Evaders who preferred jail to the Army, will remain open until better and wiser men than ourselves shall emerge who can translate into workable alternatives for tomorrow the hopes and the aspirations that aroused so much commotion only yesterday.